My Way with Trout

My Way with TROUT

ARTHUR COVE

The Crowood Press

First published in 1986 by
THE CROWOOD PRESS
Ramsbury, Marlborough
Wiltshire SN8 2HE

British Library Cataloguing in Publication Data
Cove, Arthur
My way with trout.
1. Trout fishing   2. Fly Fishing
I. Title
799.1'755   SH687
ISBN 0–946284–24–5

Acknowledgements

The publishers would like to thank Tim Daniels and Don Griggs for
their kind permission to make available the *Church Hill Farm* lakes for'
the demonstration photographs.

Thanks to Taff Price for the three chironomid drawings on page 67.

Line illustrations by Annette Findlay.

Typeset by Inforum Ltd, Portsmouth
Printed in Great Britain

Contents

Introduction

I have always been an Angler. At the age of two I fell in the Grand Union canal at Sudbury, and was fished out by my Dad who was also a good fisherman. I now realise what a lucky fellow I have been. I now know that those of us who venture forth in search of fish with a rod are drugged so much that, although trying to make a living in a normal world, we are never happier than when by the side of a vast amount of water. If the results are not all they might be, there is still great joy to be had in engaging friends in talk of what we have done and what we hope to do in future. This fatal attraction for water has taken me into many strange, beautiful and idiotic places, that I may never otherwise have seen. If I had taken up another sport, I doubt if I would have ever witnessed the most marvellous sunsets and dawnings in a vast number of different scenes. I am just as happy on a wintry shingle beach in my hunt for cod as at the mouth of some little Welsh river, attempting to catch the huge bass I know frequent these places. Whether out in a boat in salt water in pursuit of the many species I have been fortunate enough to catch, or when risking my life wading out into rivers running fast, in pursuit of the king of fish, the salmon, the satisfaction is just as great. I find even my match fishing career has helped me to master the most interesting, time absorbing pursuit of all our fish, the trout. Given the right set of circumstances, it can be the greatest fulfilment and pleasure that I could ever experience and appreciate.

One complements the other, and little things you pick up from one branch of angling can help another. I can imagine you wondering what possible connection there can be between hurtling a 5oz lead against a gale on a cod beach on the east coast and the delicate art of extracting trout from a Midland reservoir, but I will argue that the process of casting with a 12ft beachcaster is just as critical in timing as laying an ambush for a cruising trout. Also it teaches you a lot about nylon and knots, which are taken for granted by most people. Once you have been snapped off a time or two with a multiplier reel on a storm beach, you begin to make sure your knots are reliable and your timing perfect in delivery. You can also learn from the playing of the fish itself; especially in a heavy sea when you manage to get a big cod caught in the undertow and it's sucked back outwards with alarming speed. If you hadn't had

With Field-Marshall Montgomery, himself a keen angler.

the sense to ease off the drag, you would have lost it. Yes, the relevance
is there all the time for me, for even cod from a boat can give the most
delicate bite which, if I hadn't been a match fisherman, I would have
missed. Often on the so-called still waters of a trout lake, I have used
match tactics in dealing with fish which are not visible at the surface
although feeding on or near the bottom, and put many a fish in the bag.

During these many years, I've always kept my pursuit of fish as a
sport and cannot understand the present day attitude of a few, who,
after buying a ticket to fish, feel that if they don't catch the limit, they

have been cheated. I would suggest that it would be cheaper in their case to go to a fishmonger and buy their catch. For I have found that over the years, the one thing you don't want to do when fishing is put yourself into a situation where you are tense. The more relaxed you are, the better you will do, and the more confidence you will have. I know that when I go to a fishery, if given my head, the poor owner will have to restock after I am finished. In truth, I nowadays usually fish on the understanding that I can return fish to the water, but I always, *always*, read the rules of any water I go to and if I come to some private arrangement, then that's my business.

By Beachy Head with a sea bass of 12lb plus taken on a small squid.

In recent years, I have killed very few fish compared to the number I have caught and, looking back over recent seasons, I have averaged well over a thousand trout a year. To your ears this may seem impossible, especially as I rarely fish all day and much prefer to be at the water at the time when I consider that I am in with most chance. In high summer, this can be just a couple of hours late in the evening. I may get twenty or more fish quite easily in that hour or two, much I am sorry to say, to the annoyance of some people who have been there from first light. That is as it may be, but if I were those others, I would want to know the reasons why. I am of the opinion that you can never know too much, and believe me, I'm still learning. Because reservoir angling is a fairly recent branch of trout fishing, every week turns up something new for me and it is rare upon a visit to the water, that I don't learn more. The one real asset I have in my favour is the fact that I have a very good memory, which more often than not stands me in good stead.

I am not very educated as will become apparent. I am also not very technically minded, but when I get a bee in my bonnet, I will concentrate intensely to find the right answers and the best advice I can give you is to keep your eyes open. If you see something you do not understand, enquire until you get an explanation; read as much as you can. Not all the right answers are in modern books; many of the old ones are much more informative and my pride and joy is my collection of them. However, most public libraries can obtain the books you need if they have not already got them.

I have tried to put into print some of the basic problems that stillwater or reservoir fishermen are confronted with in a season's fishing, and simply explain the tackle and tactics I have used to overcome a good few of them.

It never ceases to make me wonder that most of the dedicated trout fishermen I know are just a little 'touched', and God knows I associate with quite a few of them. One I know uses dry fly only, even in early season when other methods are producing fish all around him, and it does not perturb him one bit. I suppose he has the odd session in a season when he will score over a multitude present and these odd times make his day – that's his way and I respect him for it. I dare say that some people I fish alongside think the same about me. I recall a time when fishing for salmon with the fly. I hooked a sea trout of about 4½lb and released it. My mate asked me why. I said that it wasn't the fish I was after. Looney? I think not, for it's a single minded business and when I go after a certain species of fish that's the one I want, and I know of a few other anglers who feel the same way.

Another thing I know annoys a few is the fact that sometimes when getting fish on a certain pattern of fly, I will take it off and try a completely different one. This cures a boredom which can come about when you are too successful. On quite a few occasions I have had the limit for the water in just three casts and this is soul destroying for me because I've been looking forward to a few hours' fishing, and have mucked it up in a few minutes. This is why I don't really like to go to waters on press days, or opening days, for when the fish are 'green' they are far too easy to hook and there's really no pleasure in pulling out fish after fish, which I'm sure a child could do.

I remember one well-known water having a so-called 'press day', whereupon forty or fifty well-known angling writers and 'experts' descended upon it and slaughtered fish, one after another. I arrived with John Wilshaw, then Editor of *Trout Fisherman*, about a couple of hours after the crowd, and John on his first cast hooked three fish on a team of nymphs. He turned to me, asked me to help land them and I gave my usual reply, 'You hooked 'em, you get them out!' I believe that an angler should land his own fish. We caught plenty and I remember the photographer saying to me a few hours later, 'You've had a hundred fish.' I stopped and asked what he meant and he said that he had counted all I had caught and that the last one was the hundredth. This staggered me for it seemed to be a ridiculous number, but he assured me this was so. When we finished, I found that John had killed only two fish and I three, and those only because we had to for if a fish bleeds, it's better knocked on the head. All the others went back fit and well. If you don't mess about playing to the gallery and get them in quick, with plenty of life in them, and unhook without touching them, they will swim away. If you spend a long time in playing them, they soon get exhausted, then they will die. Sad to say, most of the others went off with bags full of fish.

This sickened me so much that I haven't been to another press day since to fish seriously. I would have hated to have been a paying customer the next day when it opened to the public. Better by far to invite those same people accompanied by a novice or young angler and let the experienced men teach them a few lessons in fishing and etiquette, something in my opinion which is sadly lacking from our modern trout fishing scene.

I have attempted to put down how I started to approach trout fishing in lakes and reservoirs with simple explanations of the progress I have made. I hope you will learn just a little from the many successes I have had and avoid the mistakes I made too. This book is mainly about nymphs and larvae and pupae, but I have included a little of all those techniques which I have found useful in putting more than a few fish on the bank.

I started fishing for trout on reservoirs and still waters in 1952, having fished on rivers in Germany while serving in the Army. When I returned home I found that it was virtually impossible to find decent trout fishing in any rivers in my local area, in Northamptonshire. There were a few lakes stocked with trout in my vicinity, and at two of these I could purchase day tickets to fish which were not too expensive; namely Ravensthorpe and Eyebrook, the latter of which I instantly fell in love with. This was a lake supplying water to the Stewart & Lloyd steelworks at Corby, and was modelled on a Scottish loch, to the extent of even having Highland cattle in the land around it.

So began an obsession with reservoir trout fishing. It was then in its infancy and has expanded rapidly ever since. At that time, nobody knew that much about the feeding habits of these lowland stillwater fish and, as a raw beginner, I had to learn the hard way, because the accepted way of fishing was mainly composed of the traditional method of loch fishing with traditional flies. I must confess that for a dozen visits to Eyebrook, I wasn't very successful. At this time it was stocked with brown trout only and they were very difficult indeed. I remember one day during this early period at Eyebrook seeing another angler catch a brace of nice fish. On walking up the hundred yards or so to ask him what was his successful fly, he hid his flies in the palm of his hand and told me to find out, the same as he had done. You must understand that at this time, if there were a dozen anglers fishing the whole of the water it was crowded, and if you wanted to fish close to another angler (close was 30yds), you asked his permission first.

Happily, times have changed and nowadays if you ask how your near neighbours are catching they will usually tell you the fly and the method. If they tie their own, they *might* give you the successful fly as well. I did learn, and from the very beginning I took the trouble to examine the contents of trouts' stomachs and came to the conclusion that ninety-five per cent or so of the stomachs I examined were full of nymphs and larvae of one description or another, plus certain beetles, shrimps and snails and a certain number of coarse fish fry.

These observations have proved invaluable over the years and I am firmly of the opinion that dedicated anglers should keep notes of weather, temperatures, water and overhead conditions to assist them on later expeditions.

In 1953, it was not possible to go into a tackle shop and buy imitations of the 'things' I found in trouts' stomachs. So I decided to try and tie some myself, buying a cheap vice and some Pearsalls tying silk. I embarked upon a study to try to copy them accurately and soon found out that this was much easier said than done. Yes, I still remember studying a nymph or bug in a glass bottle, spending half an hour or so making a passable copy, and then having the silk break when tying it off at the head and seeing the whole thing slowly unwind from the hook shank. There was many a time that the fly tying gear came very close to being thrown through the window.

However, I persevered and eventually started to turn out reasonable copies. I would like to say that I had instant success at fooling the fish into taking them, but this was not to be so. Although I was much more successful at prising fish out of Eyebrook than other anglers, I was not satisfied with the results after covering a lot of fish. I came to the conclusion that, although my copies were passable to me, probably the methods of fishing them were not quite right. In the following season I started to experiment with different types of retrieves and presentation and was much more successful. My bag rate was rising so rapidly that people were saying all the usual things about worms and maggots. I remember vividly the manager of the fishery, Mr Robinson, springing to my defence, saying one evening after weighing in nineteen trout after a few hours' fishing time (when the bag was usually a brace to a brace and a half), that probably the most sporting angler on the lake was myself. I felt immensely pleased and moved on in leaps and bounds, sometimes catching thirty to forty trout in a day's fishing (naturally not killing all of them, even though there was no limit in those days). I then started to spend a lot of time studying these nymphs and bugs in their own environment. I watched how they moved and tried to copy their movement with different types of retrieve until I started to get it near enough right.

I strongly believe that you should observe all that happens around you when spending time at the water. Once you learn the sequence of events on one particular water, you are well on the way to knowing the imitations to use at a particular time on most other lakes in the area, even though they may vary slightly by a week or two. In early season weather conditions are important, but the further south the water, the earlier the hatch – a distance of twenty miles can make a week's difference in April. You may well question the sense in using nymphs and pupae under cold conditions, but as long as there is some open water, even if a lake is iced up, there is usually a hatch of some description. The fact is that I find using nymphs and larvae is the most

Tom Ivens, like Arthur Cove, an early pioneer of stillwater trout fishing.

efficient way of catching fish, as opposed to fishing lures and fry imitations which, in my experience, have a very limited use. I don't intend to make this a contribution to the nymph versus lure fishing argument. I too have passed through the lure fishing stage and could probably teach quite a few lessons on this branch of trout catching; but I won't.

I must end this introduction with a story that will endorse the efficiency of using nymphs under the most trying conditions you are likely to meet.

A few years ago, while attending a 'teach in' run by *Trout Fisherman* magazine at Pateshall Park, a class of mainly experienced anglers asked me if it was possible to catch trout under the conditions prevailing at the time. Most of the lake was covered in ice of up to two inches thick. I saw the disbelief on their faces when I said that it was possible if I could get my nymphs into the water.

The following morning it was just as cold, and the staff of the fishery spent a long time breaking the ice to allow the boats to go out (I still think those chaps were putting their lives at risk). After breakfast, a few of the chaps asked me if I really thought that I would fulfil the promise I had made the night before and I said 'Yes, but I am going to wait until the conditions are right or as right as they are likely to get.' While most of the others ventured forth on boats, I sat in the warm dining room until about 11.30am, watching them struggle. I decided this was the time to make my move. From now till about 2.00pm it was as warm as it was going to get, so I picked up my tackle and wandered off down the lake, with a few chaps in tow, to a bridge going over the neck of a bay at the far end. The ice had been broken by the boat which had come out that morning to clear the ice for the other boats. Tackling up quickly, I put on a size eight longshank Stick Fly on point, a size ten Pheasant Tail on first dropper and a size twelve Black Spider on the top dropper. I annointed my leader, which was 18ft long, with a sinking compound, cast in and waited a couple of minutes to let the flies sink well down and started to retrieve as slowly as I possibly could. On the second retrieve I had a beautiful slow draw, lifted and was into my first fish, a nice rainbow, about 1½lb. I continued fishing until about 2.00pm and finished up with eleven nice fish, probably more than the rest of the course put together. Everyone seemed to be most impressed apart from myself, for I knew that I had missed quite a few, owing to my slow re-actions due to the gallery talking to me as I fished. I remember one of the bailiffs at Grafham telling me some time before he knew how to stop me catching fish, by talking to me, causing a lapse in concentration.

Fishing to the gallery at Pattershall Park. Though there was only a
small channel in the ice below, the nymphs caught fish that day.

The first lesson is that the takes are usually so light under difficult
conditions that you cannot relax for a moment and all the indications
you are likely to get are a one or two inch dip on the end of the line. If
you lift at this precise moment, the fish is more often than not well
hooked. The other lesson is doing your homework, in this case asking
the bailiffs where I could get over water not more than 10ft deep, to
allow me to scrape the Stick Fly over a relatively clean bottom. I also
realised that there was a very good hatch of sedges at the appropriate
time of the season, ensuring that the caddis larvae would be plentiful.
Suffice it to say that I had fish on all the patterns I used on the leader
that morning. But by far the most productive was the Stick Fly. Oh yes,
and the final lesson, picking the most productive time to fish.
   I must add that during my years at the Grafham Water Education

Early days at Grafham. These were all taken on a Pheasant Tail
Nymph.

Centre courses, I became deeply indebted to all the instructors for the
advice and help freely given. All of them were World or National
Champions and I now know what a lucky fellow I was. People used to
tell me at the end of the course that they had learnt more in the
weekend than they had done in a lifetime's fishing. If you tried to pick
a list of instructors better than these guys, I'm sure you would be very
hard pushed.

Don Neish – probably the smoothest and most stylish caster I have ever known. Also a brilliant engineer.

Ian Blagburn – a canny Scot, quite happy with three or four rods in each hand. He could have kept a bunch of trout anglers occupied, him casting, them doing the fishing.

Mike Weddel – a joy to watch and so dedicated. He could stand ten yards behind me and outcast me by a distance.

Dick Swift – no longer with us I am sad to say. I learnt a lot from him. He was a man of great patience with me and taught me a hell of a lot of tricks to use when fishing. All the others used to say of him, 'If Dick hits one right, it's goodbye trophy.' What an epitaph.

They, having seen me fish, would discuss my style and I can assure you their remarks weren't very complimentary. But they all agreed, although I casted, as one put it, 'like a crippled cow', I got it out there with good presentation and, most important, caught fish.

I wish I had known then what I know now. I could have probably made my discussions sound a little more convincing. Even in those days I used very long leaders with a team of flies and know that it's much easier to make casting look nicer with a short leader and keeping the line in a tight loop. With these long leaders and a team of flies, you have to master casting with a wide loop or you'll be in a tangle every two minutes.

Happy days, those at Grafham, and I'm sure we all learnt a lot from one another. By the way, I used to instruct on tactics, and I'm still learning.

I will now explain the tackle I use and how to set it up, and run through a session from start to finish. I shall also attempt to explain the basic approach to nymph fishing and how to use it effectively. You will be surprised how few patterns of nymph you will need. No doubt for a start you will find it hard going, but I guarantee that once you master it, you will not feel satisfied fishing in any other way. I hope that you can learn to stand still and do nothing – the hardest part for anglers.

1 Equipment and Technique

Rods

I often get asked what the perfect rod for trout fishing would be like if I was able to design it. After thinking about it I came to the conclusion that the question is much the same as asking 'How long is a piece of string?' Mr Average Angler wants a rod that will cast out of sight, be able to hook fish efficiently at a great multitude of ranges with hooks varying in size from sixes down to twenties. You can take it from me that *that* rod has never come on the market and I don't think it ever will. So, coming to this unhappy conclusion, I would make the observation that we must either compromise or do as a few chaps I know, who go out trout fishing with as many rods as a golfer has clubs in his bag. I am neither inclined to take a caddie along with me nor be cluttered up with all that tackle. If I accepted all I read in the adverts, I'm sure I could fill a lorry with all the rods which I am supposed to have.

I started at the end of the built cane/silk line era and I have been fortunate enough to obtain and use most of the rods made up to the present day. I reckon I've got more qualifications than most for commenting on the types of rod that are useful and those that are not. I will say one thing about the built cane rods that we used in those days, that those made by the most famous makers were very much like one another in action in their types. By this I mean that I could pick up two rods in the same name, say a Hardy Pope 10ft, and they were much like each other. This is more than I could have said when they started to supply fibreglass rods. The variation was brought home to me one evening when fishing at Grafham with a certain well-known reservoir rod and a chap next to me said 'I can't get my line out as far as you.' I knew that he had the same rod as myself and I asked him if I could fish with his tackle which he instantly handed over. His rod was twice as stiff as the one I had. The next day I checked on the half dozen rods of that make in the shop and found that they all varied in action – disconcerting to say the least. Of course, those old cane rods were all tested by weighting the tip against a graph on a wall jig and if they did not come within certain tolerances they were rejected. This is what I was told and I had no reason to disbelieve it, but I doubt if any

Arthur Cove with his favourite 'Grafham Ghost', the first really good
purpose-built reservoir trout rod. Note the difference in diameter
between the old 'Grafham Ghost' and the modern boron rod
(below).

manufacturer still does it today.

So, whatever type of rod you are after, it will pay you to take your reel and line with you and put it through its paces before you buy, and most good tackle shops will allow you to do this.

In fact what usually happens is that you go to a shop and buy a rod which is, say, an AFTM seven, marked 7 on the butt and if you are a beginner, fix it up with a size seven system line. You go out with a mate, get a little instruction and start to fish, and this usually works well for about half a dozen sessions. Then, as you get a bit more proficient in casting, you find your rod usually starts to lose power and it's just not true at all. But a few manufacturers explain that with the AFTM system (which is universal), the weight-number system is calculated over the first 30ft of line. Now you don't need me to tell you that this is 10yds of line, and our beginner has improved his casting and is probably using 15 to 18yds of line and is therefore overloading his rod. My cure for this situation is to drop a line size and go down to a number six or even a size five, and I am referring to double taper lines.

One of the more amusing things that happened during the development of fibreglass rods was the way in which most manufacturers were stressing the lightness of their product and adding to the weight of fixtures and fittings, some of them with metal ferrules and heavy reel fittings, and also some with solid glass ferrules. The first really light rod produced during this period was the Grafham Ghost. This was a 9½ft two piece with hollow glass spigot ferrule, aluminium butt cap and ring reel fitting with the best snake rings available. This rod was a dream to use and I found no trouble putting out a double taper five or six line all the way. With a shooting head of 42½ft of No. 6 with nylon backing, I consistently put out 50yds with a wind at the back. This rod was produced by Don Neish of Don's of Edmonton. It weighed just 4½oz and the action was progressive from the tip down and when you hooked a fish, the whole rod came into play. I do not think I ever had an anxious moment while using this rod, even when jumping big fish over the sticks of half sunken hedgerows. It was nice to be full of confidence. I wish I still had the rod – hope the bloke who borrowed it reads this, I'd love to have it back!

However, time marches on, and a few years later Don Neish showed me a 9½ft carbon fibre blank imported from America. I was very impressed with its diameters and power, and it was not long before he had made me a rod out of it. This was the Graphlex, and although it took me a couple of sessions to get used to, it fitted nicely into my style of fishing. Although I could not cast any further with it than with the Ghost, it had definite advantages in being much easier to cast into a strong headwind, due no doubt to its very fine (for then) diameter.

At this period, many types of carbons and carbon fibreglass rods started to appear. All sorts of claims were being made and some even confused the AFTM system by claiming that certain rods would handle from number five to eleven system lines – and of course they would. A broomstick will do exactly the same in the right hands, but not efficiently. But I don't want to fish with a broomstick so I look for a rod that will cast reasonably well. I've long ago given up struggling to push a line out so far that I could not possibly expect to hook and hold a fish. I concentrate far more now on perfect presentation for, believe me, you'll get more fish at close range than you ever get at distance. It's my opinion that it's the angler who drives the fish out by shoddy presentation and wading out too far, pushing the fish even further away. Remember that the bulk of a trout's food comes from the warmer shallow water around the sides of most lakes and it doesn't really take water of any great depth to cover even a ten pounder's back. I have hooked fish of 8lb plus in less than a foot's depth. In some ways, we anglers are our own worst enemies – over a good many years now we have been striving for lighter rods, and God forbid we should return to the 10ft built cane rods which I started with, weighing 12 to 14oz or more. I would now like to make a suggestion that might surprise more than a few, in the statement that the weight of a rod has very little to do with the problems of fatigue. I've read about early fishermen using trout rods of 18ft in length and I've seen A.E.H. Wood use a 12ft built cane rod while greased line fishing on the Dee in a marvellous old film of Hardy's, single handed I might add. I made a joke about the action of the rod as he cast across the fast running river – it was as soft as a wet week. I remember picking up a tournament casting rod of Mike Weddel's at one of the trout fishing courses at Grafham Water Education Centre, it being so powerful that I could only manage one false cast with it. The fact is that I got 64m and Mike told me not to take up tournament casting because with practice, I might get better. I didn't tell him that if I had tried to do two false casts, it would have broken my arm.

It seems to me that those old guys knew more about balance than we give them credit for. I have an old Hardy 18ft salmon rod that can pick up forty yards of line and put it back across the river with only a fraction of effort from me. In fact, it's only a matter of leaning back and waiting till the line straightens out behind and then leaning forward and

In full cry!

following the line down with the rod tip till it lights on the water. That rod does ninety per cent of the work for me and this is what I want my ideal trout rod to do; most of the work with minimum effort, without being so soft it won't lift a high line without effort. The rod must develop its flexibility from the tip downwards.

So now we have this blank, what sort of fittings are we going to use? Well, I would go for a nice slim cork handle with a Dural butt cap and ring fitting, not being a great lover of screw reel fittings, although I know that the good ones are made of nylon material these days. I prefer the slim cork handle because most handles are far too fat and you can lose a lot of effort through this padding before it's transferred to the blank. In fact a lot of tournament casters used to shape the cork so their thumb was actually pushing against the bare glass, and in a competition where less than a foot was the difference between winning and losing, I can understand why.

Of all the rings available, including the latest Fuji rings, the good quality snake ring is still the best and Don Neish produces the best I know of. I would plump for a lined butt ring and the lightest tip ring available, but, as was pointed out to me a long time ago, it's possible to change the action of the blank completely by using heavy rings.

No rings could get worse treatment than mine and you will understand later the reason why I've only had one new set in ten years. The best tip I can give you is to clean the rod and rings thoroughly once a week during the season with a mixture of warm water and a little detergent, paying particular attention to the rings themselves.

One final word on the rod. Over the years I have found that the length of 9½ft is my ideal size because, with practice, it will throw a reasonably high line behind and is long enough with the action to be useful when fishing over or through bankside weed, and it will also double as an occasional boat rod. Yes, I can hear your brains ticking over and thinking that a longer rod will throw a higher line. Of course this would make life a lot simpler if it was true. Many of the people I knew found this out when Grafham Dam first opened to fishing, and we all left our fair share of flies at the back of the wall. I remember hearing them say that they wanted a longer rod to clear it, and upon getting one, they proceeded to hit the wall lower down than before. What was happening was that these rods were flexing more and they were actually putting their back-cast lower down. Remember, it's where you check the tip of the rod on the throw back that determines whether the line goes high or low. The further forward you check, the higher it goes. Once you have checked and the line is straightening, you can follow the line back with the tip to get a long pull forward to achieve maximum distance. Ten minutes with a competent instructor will do a power of good!

Altogether the rod must be a compromise of many things and one good guide must be that if it feels comfortable, delivers your flies at the right place and time with good presentation and handles a fish well, then it is the right one for you. Be prepared to sacrifice a little distance to achieve this and I think you will find, as I have over the years, it will put a lot more fish in the bag. Buy the best rod you can afford – you don't get quality cheap. When you've got your rod buy a hard case to keep it in; mine are made of strong plastic. More rods are broken in boots and car doors than in fishing. Look after it, keep it clean and it should last you a lifetime. Inspect the rings at regular intervals and if they show signs of wear, renew them instantly. I've seen lines stripped of their plastic coatings in less than a day's fishing with a grooved ring.

Reels

I think the most important factor in matching a reel to a rod is to achieve a balance between the two so that they complement each other. They are going to spend a lot of time teamed together in your hands and if one doesn't combine with the other, it makes for a very uncomfortable union. It is possible to have a reel too light for a rod, which in some cases makes a rod feel tip heavy, and this can be very tiresome. Better by far to have more weight at the butt end which will make the whole outfit feel much more comfortable.

Whether you pick a single action reel or multiplier depends on which way you prefer to play your fish. I confess I prefer the multiplier for the very simple reason I like to play the fish from the reel as soon as possible. I am sure you will find, as I have done, that when you hand line a fish in, the line is usually pulled through the butt ring into a heap in front of you, either in the water or on the bank. It invariably finishes up under your feet, squashed into the mud, sand and grit, which shortens the life of your fly line considerably and furthermore catches on the weeds, twigs and sometimes rocks or stones as you back out to land the fish. I have seen the situation quite a few times when an angler, while playing a trout, has allowed the line he has retrieved to be blown downwind for some considerable distance and the fish, when on his short and curlies, has jumped through this line dangling between his reel and butt ring. I remember one angler asking me what he should do – and getting the quick answer to leave it alone, it might hang itself!

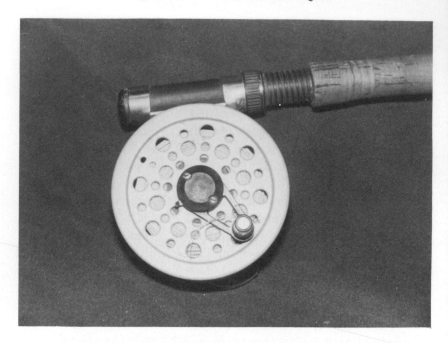

The multiplier reel (above) will recover line about two and a half times faster than the single action reel (below) but it will not last as long.

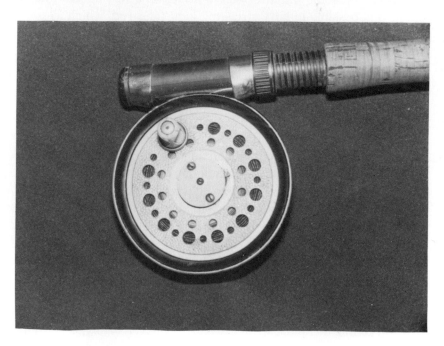

Into a late evening fish at Ringstead.

This is how I manage my own fish. When retrieving and I get a take, I generally finish up with the line in a coil in my left hand. I grip this coil and lift the rod until I feel the fish, then I hold it firmly until I am sure the hook is well home. Usually the fish doesn't do a thing except shake his head. I then throw the coil of line I had in my left hand on the water in front of me and start to get the line onto the reel. In practice, the hooked fish doesn't seem to move far until I catch up with him, and by this time I have no slack line between butt ring and reel at all. From now on the play is normal but all the line is safely on the reel.

The advantage of the multiplier is its speed in getting the line back on the spool, but I must stress that it must be steered back on and not allowed to run onto one side or the other, building up to tangle itself. After a little bit of practice, this becomes easy. One further small problem is that when packing up, some anglers leave their leader attached to their butt piece at the end of the line. Take my advice – don't. The nylon will surely tuck itself between the coils of fly line already on the spool and you will have the devil's own job of trying to find the end again. If this does happen, the quickest and best way to rectify the problem is to take the spool off the reel. If the worst comes to the worst, make sure you can recognise the leader material before you start tugging at it. Nylon can cut a fly line too.

Practise getting the line to finish in the palm of the hand as a coil rather than a figure of eight.

Casting from a coil in the hand allows you to get line out quickly, as well as avoiding frustrating tangles on the ground.

With all its little problems, the multiplier pays for itself in efficiency and speed. Of those I have used, I have found the Shakespeare 3½in wide spool Speedex to be most reliable. The single action reels I use are always the type where the spool can be taken off instantly. Other points to watch for are badly fitting spools and sharp edges, mainly on the line guards, which can catch the line.

The reel is probably the item of tackle that gets misused the most. It usually gets put down on the muddy ground when dispatching a fish, and a few moments later is having line snatched off it furiously to cover another fish. If, as often happens, you hear a grating sound when attempting to pull line off or when trying to wind in, dip it into the water and agitate. This will usually clear it, but don't forget to wash it and lightly oil after a session. It's annoying how much muck they can collect. The one I am using at present is ten seasons old and is still in perfect nick.

You might ask 'Why a 3½in wide spool reel?' Well, for my style of fishing it is going to hold a full double taper line, plus a hundred yards of braided backing, and you will find that the narrow spool reels just don't have the capacity to carry all this. If you want to be really versatile, you'll need two spare spools.

Backing

I much prefer the braided type of backing because it is virtually indestructible, doesn't stretch much and lasts, with care, for years and years. In fact, the backing on one of my reels is the same I started with over thirty years ago and it's still like new. I dare say it would probably cost a hell of a lot more now than I paid for it.

One word of warning if you do use nylon backing for shooting heads or for any type of line. Make sure you put on some soft material that will cushion it and give, for many spools have been broken because of the elasticity of nylon when wound on under pressure. It is a good idea to change nylon backing frequently owing to its rapid loss of strength when exposed to sunlight. Also, if you use the flat type backing for shooting heads, don't put more than fifty yards on the spool. I doubt if you'll use more than this in actual fishing. Keep the rest in a bag or something in a cool dark place; it keeps longer in good condition this way.

Fly Lines

Fly lines are probably the most important of all the equipment used, for without a carefully chosen line, the best of rods cannot perform to the perfection needed to be consistent in placing your flies accurately and with minimum effort. Although most fly lines look the same when handed over the counter at your tackle shop, they are as different as chalk to cheese. They don't reveal their true characteristics until you have put them through their paces over a few fishing sessions. It's false economy to buy mill ends and some of the cheaper lines that are advertised with all their irregularities, poor finish and uneven weights and tapers. I find it is cheaper by far to buy the very best quality available and take the brand of line where the quality control and production are perfect.

I well remember being sent a sample of two lines to try some years ago. After fishing a couple of times with them unsatisfactorily, I made a close inspection of them and was astonished to find that the surfaces of both lines were so uneven it was ridiculous. I rang up the Managing Director and pointed this out to him. 'Oh yes,' he said, 'we make them like that. Fly lines travel very fast you know and we find that like this, they go through the rings better.' So I asked him 'If that's the case, then why isn't Concorde corrugated?' Well I am like that anyway – they went back by return post.

Virtually all lines at present on the market are made of a level core of braided synthetic fibre, covered by a dressing of polyvinyl chloride. This covering is treated in various ways to provide different degrees of density to make the lines sink at different rates. The floating lines have tiny air bubbles in this outer coat to make them float and the sinkers generally incorporate a metallic dust in this coat to get a carefully calculated increased density. Sometimes they combine to give lines that float in some parts and sink in others.

DOUBLE TAPER

Of course there are many types of line but for my style of fishing I prefer the double taper. This line consists of a level belly section with identical tapers at each end. The tapered section varies from 8 to 12ft depending on the size of the line and manufacturer's design. This is probably one of the oldest forms of line and is invaluable in that it is satisfactory for moderate distance and works with dry fly, wet fly and nymphs. It will roll, cast and allow you to mend line and, by far its most important attribute, it can be used for changing direction very quickly.

It's usually about thirty yards long and is most sensitive when feeling for takes, and in floating form with a slight modification, it can be invaluable in being easily seen when you master my method of nymph fishing. The floater is, owing to its construction, in the form of a slight sink tip. Being tapered, the front portion does not have the capacity to hold many air bubbles, so consequently after a few minutes' use, it tends to sink, and this can be a problem under some conditions.

This can of course be rectified quite easily with Permaflote. You will find me recommending these line treatments very often but I can assure you I have no interest in promoting their sale. The fact is as far as I am concerned, they are the best available:

Permaplas which is a fly line-replasticiser.
Permaflote makes dry flies float like corks.
Permagrease is very useful for making line or leader float.

I cannot let this opportunity pass without commenting on the other types of line available having at one time or another used them.

FORWARD TAPER LINES

These consist of a heavy forward portion, tapered at the front with a thin running line behind, with sometimes a swelled portion which, when it comes to hand, indicates that the heavy forward part is clear of the tip ring.

The dressed running line is more manageable than most other backing lines but is subject to rapid wear when used with a double haul technique. This running line is usually more manageable than the nylon backing used with shooting heads. The one real advantage in this line is the ease of handling and lack of joins in the length of line.

I have found out, after long experience, that usually one can achieve a maximum distance with it with ease but try to force another few yards and, for me, it collapses in a heap at the business end. Presentation, unless you know how to control the shoot, can be dodgy. Once into the delivery, it is very difficult to change direction.

There are quite a few variations in this line, including the long belly which has a much longer forward section to give increased distance to expert casters. Also there is the nymph tip line which is a forward taper line with an additional swelled section of fluorescent red at the front end to make it easily seen. Presentation in this line I have found to be poor. Once when fishing on Lough Melvin in Ireland, I was using a double taper green coloured line. My mate was using this nymph tip. Fish after fish came up and inspected this piece of fluorescent line while I was catching every fish that moved. Upon telling him, he instantly chopped it off, retied his butt piece and leader with the same flies, and started to get fish instantly. We saw it floating in the late evening with trout still coming up to look at it! I hope Dennis doesn't mind me telling this story; well, he did get the biggest fish, a nice char about three pounds. The most beautiful I've ever seen – first bloke I've ever seen kiss a fish! We should have had it set up but I gave it to a farmer for breakfast and I have a suspicion that 'D' still hasn't forgiven me.

SINK TIP

These lines are usually any permutation of the aforementioned, where the main part of the thick belly is a floater, while a portion at the front end is of increased density so that it will sink to enable the fly to be fished at varying depths. In all, the casting qualities are not very good, owing to the dense section at the front. There are more subtle ways of getting a fly to fish deeper.

NEUTRAL DENSITY

I must confess, I had great hopes when this line became available, for it would have filled a big hole in my armoury of nymph fishing under the most trying conditions – the flat calm. When I got one I was most disappointed to find that the front end tended to float while the back end sank. I decided to reverse it (it being a double taper), and found that exactly the same thing happened. So I was forced to return to the original line I used under these conditions and furthermore, upon talking to quite a few other anglers who had tried them, was not surprised to hear that they had had the same experience. Don't waste your money, I'll tell you later how to sort out flat calms.

SINKING LINES

There are many variations of sinking lines, including slow sinkers, fast sinkers, high density, head core and all points in between. To me nowadays, apart from salmon fishing, I have very little use for a sinking line of any description, but I must give credit to their usefulness as I did use them quite effectively in my earlier days. Although I don't very often carry one with me now, I will still use one on very rare occasions. For given the right conditions, they will produce a lot of fish in a short time.

I must also explain straight away that these lines will, owing to their density, push very efficiently into quite a strong wind far more easily than a floating line will ever do; hence the use mainly of high density lines for tournament casting.

I think most of us when starting used to carry two rods, one made up with a sinker. I'll tell you a story. When Chew Valley was opened to the public for trout fishing, word filtered back to us of the very good quality trout being taken there. A good friend of mine, Bob Bridgeman, who had the fishing tackle shop in Witney, Oxfordshire, offered to show me around. He asked me to meet him at the lodge at 6.00am on the Sunday, but I told him I was not going to be able to get there at that unearthly hour and that I would meet him there nearer 10.00am – after all, it was over one hundred and thirty miles from our place. He warned me it would be crowded and I took no notice, eventually arriving at 10.15. Upon purchasing our tickets (I had brought a friend with me), we looked out, and naturally they were shoulder to shoulder as far as the eye could see. We got back into the car, not seeing Bob in the vicinity, and drove down the road towards Bishop Sutton. When we came close to the lake, we stopped and got out with tackle. We proceeded over the fence to find just one fishing spot about two hundred yards away to the right. I told my friend to nip up and get in quick which he did, me being left standing looking down a narrow ditch that went into the lake about forty yards from me, wondering what to do.

I stood in this position for about three minutes, looking right and left, when all of a sudden I heard and saw a slight disturbance in this ditch and, thinking to myself that it couldn't have been a fish, I started to keep a closer watch on it. Believe me, it was so narrow that I could see where other anglers going up the bank had stepped across it and furthermore, there were two blokes fishing just a few yards from where it entered the main water. After a few more minutes I saw another movement about twenty yards from me. I looked closer into this ditch and saw that it had a clean silt bottom with marks in this silt where caddis had been crawling. I decided to give it a go.

There was a stiff breeze blowing up this ditch which, where I stood, was about two feet deep, getting deeper as it went down. In the interest of accuracy, I picked up the rod with the sinking line attached, tied on two Stick Flies and a Corixa on top dropper and tried a chuck of about twenty yards down it. I let everything settle for a minute or two, tweaked the line twice, the line tightened up and a brownie of about 3½lb jumped straight out of the water onto the mud. I dashed down and collared it, and got back to my rod complete with fish. After straightening everything out again, I put the line once again down the ditch and hey presto, another coconut! This continued for the next couple of hours or so (no limits in those days) until I heard two blokes talking, coming down the bank from my left and, seeing one of them was Bob, I waited for them to get to me. I'll never forget what he said to the chap he was with, 'There you are Gordon, I told you it was him. He's the only looney bugger I know who would fish in a spot like that.'

Well, with about forty good browns between about two to four and a half pounds with no trouble at all, they can put me in the 'bin' as soon as they like. Looking back, I don't think I would have been so accurate and quick at getting on to them without that sinking line. The real cruncher was that the two blokes at the end of the ditch, fishing into the lake, didn't touch a fish. Such is the stuff that reputations are made of and I don't pass many ditches without having a very good look into them. I spoke to a fair few anglers in the vicinity, 'putting them straight' as I say, and made quite a few new friends. One of them said to me, 'Fancy coming all this way for trout fishing.' I had the opportunity some years later when Grafham opened to say the same thing to the same fellow. Needless to say, we did travel down to Chew Valley and Blagdon a lot in those years and that sinking line featured prominently in my tactics. In most places there was a clean bottom where you could let your line lie before you started to perform, without the fear of getting tangled up with weed as soon as you started to retrieve. Alas, quite a lot of weed has grown over most of it now and we have to use other methods, but on brand new waters the sinking line still works well. Another situation where I find it useful is in the smaller type fisheries where I have been fishing for the last few years. There it is possible to stalk the larger fish by sight. It can be very difficult to cast accurately with very heavy nymphs with long leaders at fish you can see either sitting or cruising very deep. In this case you react to the take by actually watching the fish take your offering.

SHOOTING HEADS

Way back while in Germany, I used to get hold of the American magazines *Outdoor Life* and *Field & Stream* off some of our colonial cousins. I remember reading an article about how some of their anglers were using nylon as backing to achieve distance when fishing for steelhead in their big rivers and stored it away in my memory for future reference.

After fishing for a few years at Eyebrook, I decided to try it, and after chopping off a length of silk line (we only had silk lines at this time) and experimenting with it, found out I could cast a hell of a way, fifty yards or so, with an Iven's Ravensthorpe rod which I was using at the time. Not knowing any better, I was using 8lb breaking strain nylon as the running line. I managed to hook a few fish with it, finding that I could get a lot of pulls but that not many stayed on. I only used it at that portion of the day when things were reasonably quiet, to chuck at the occasional fish which normally rose during the day at ranges a bit more extreme than my normal tackle could manage. I remember standing talking to a chap named George who worked at Stewart & Lloyds, when a fish showed about forty-five yards out. Getting down to the water and covering it first chuck on a Green and Yellow Nymph, the fish took in a big boil and stayed stuck. I turned round and saw George, a great hairy old Scot, virtually doing handstands and muttering 'What a cast! What a cast!' When I landed the fish, a great golden brownie of about 3lb, he looked at the tackle, got out his penknife, chopped his line in half before I could stop him and told me to tie it on the same as mine. Not much I could do under the circumstances, but at least he had another reel and line, for he was a keen boat fisherman. He was a traditional and didn't fish much from the bank in any case – damn good job he didn't.

These experiences were to stand me in very good stead later on when plastic lines became available because I found that when using the silk lines which had to be greased to float, they actually floated *on* the surface and not *in the* surface as a modern floating line does. Consequently they gave far less resistance to the take of a fish, because the line skimmed across the top when a fish moved off with the offering before the front end of the line started to disappear downwards. Nevertheless, quite a lot of really good takes were missed with this early shooting head rig, no doubt due to the elasticity of the light nylon running line. I remember as well the number of tangles I used to endure. It was quite a few years until the shooting head proper came into its own, first at Chew Valley, then more popularly at Grafham Water. At the same time, I found out that in my case, 20lb nylon backing was about right. It was a couple more years afterwards that Don Neish came up with a flat nylon backing for it which floated better and stayed straighter than normal round section nylon. I think then the length of a piece of double taper line to be used was nearly always ten yards of 7-8-9-10 and sometimes even No.11. This was accepted as the right length to use with any outfit both in floating and sinking form. Very efficient they were with big flies and great big fish to wallop them, and in the first couple of years at Grafham, woe betide any angler who didn't use powerful leaders, good hooks and plenty of backing. Those

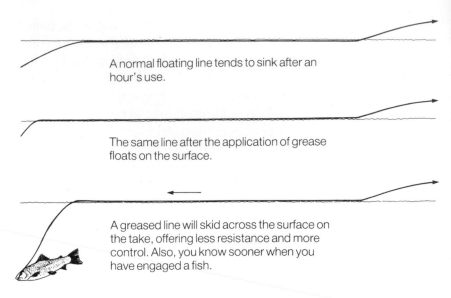

A normal floating line tends to sink after an hour's use.

The same line after the application of grease floats on the surface.

A greased line will skid across the surface on the take, offering less resistance and more control. Also, you know sooner when you have engaged a fish.

Fig 1   **The effect of greasing the line**

fish could smash 8lb nylon and a lot of the anglers didn't even know it had happened until they lifted the line out of the water.

I remember standing on the point at Savages Creek one evening with Rod Barley and George Sumpter, seeing a chap in a black Homburg, fawn mac, black trousers and a pair of bike clips, coming up to us holding a delightful little cane rod with a pretty little reel that must have held at most twenty yards of backing. He approached me asking how it was going and I told him he could fish from my spot because I had got my 'whack'. Furthermore I advised him to use my spare rod as I didn't think his was man enough for the job. Indignantly refusing the offer and standing by the water with his left hand in his mac pocket, he flicked his dry Wickham's quite nicely on the water about fifteen yards out – pretty to watch. I stood by the side of George, drinking a cup of tea, when all of a sudden there was a squeal of line being snatched. A huge rainbow leapt out of the water forty yards away and, after a clap like a rifle shot, there came a string of abuse that was an education to my ears (being an old army man). He used words I hadn't even thought of. It was away with his line, backing, the lot. He stood for a few moments looking at the water so I walked up to him, picked up my spare rod and told him I was off and if he would be so kind as to leave my rod with George Faithfull, the Head Bailiff at the lodge, I'd pick it up the next day.

Rodney and myself walked along to the car park at Hill Farm where there was a beautiful black Austin limousine with the chauffeur sitting on the wing, and as we passed he asked if we had seen his boss, describing the fellow I had lent my rod to. Being curious after telling him he was still fishing, I asked who he was. 'Oh' he replied, 'he's the Bishop of——.' Cross my heart, this, as all my stories, is absolutely true and I often wonder if he ever got to heaven. I know from the message I got when I picked up my rod the next day that he had had a nice catch of fish. Much tackle was lost, even whole lots of rods, reels and line being snatched if you were stupid enough to leave your flies dangling in the water and not only from boats, it even happened to bank anglers.

After the second season there, the fish started to get a bit clued up and the softly softly approach was producing the results for me although lures still produced a fair number of fish. At this time I met up with Dick Swift and after fishing with him quite a lot, we used to discuss the problems that I thought relevant. The main one in my case was presentation and the fact that the water was heavily fished from the bank and with anglers, including myself, wading out as far as they possibly could, we were driving the bulk of the better fish further and further away. Many articles were written at the time and I well remember one particular piece where the so-called expert described his shooting head flashing out in a sheet of spray. I pointed out to Dick that this was one of the main problems with the heads we then used. Even with great care the sevens head I was using, even though I knew how to control it by feathering the backing as it shot through the butt ring, allowing the head to straighten and leader to fall straight, was not to my satisfaction. Dick then explained to me that the 30ft of No.7 line could be improved by using 42½ft of No.6 line which would weigh roughly the same and, as when I used a full line, I could false cast a fair amount. In any case, I could achieve the same distance with better presentation. It made sense but I pointed out the one snag I could see with it, and explained that sometimes these fish would follow a team of nymphs a long way and usually if they were in this mood, they would take in the last couple of yards and with fourteen yards or more of line outside the top ring, I would be lifting off before these followers had the chance to take. Dick said 'Let's make one up for you and I'll show you how to hook the followers.'

We proceeded to make this one up and, sure enough, it was a vast improvement. With a little tuition from Dick and Don Neish, a following breeze and projecting it slightly upwards on delivery, it carried very well indeed and with good control of the backing, it straightened out nicely and landed very featherlike – just what I wanted.

Then Dick proceeded to show me how to retrieve the line to the tip ring and fetch it in further by lifting the rod and fetching in the line as though starting to do a roll cast. Being worried, I asked him what I could do if a fish took with all this slack line. He said 'Roll your line forward as if you were going to roll cast, that'll hook 'em,' and sure enough he was right. I still catch many fish this way, even with a full line. If a fish doesn't follow you, just roll cast the line into the air and proceed with the delivery. One more false cast and you can send it on its way. It's a very economical way of fishing, but once again it is limited, owing to not being able to change direction, and is not as accurate as the double taper.

COLOUR

Before finishing the main part on fly lines, I must mention that the one thing that seems to cause most controversy is the colour of the line itself. By this I mean floating lines in the main. A lot of people ask if it makes any difference and of course I answer 'Yes' as far as the fisherman is concerned and 'No' as far as the fish are concerned.

The one object of using a coloured line is to enable the angler to see it clearly and if you can see it down to the far end, the better will be the results. The one sure way of getting the right colour without buying every shade available is to go for a walk around your local water when there are a fair few people fishing. Nearly every angler there will probably have a different colour and it's up to you to decide which colour suits your eyes the best under those conditions.

As far as the fish are concerned, I suppose I have fished more lakes than most in the British Isles and Ireland and have never felt, even while fishing in brilliant sunshine in the clear chalk-lakes of southern England, that it's been a handicap fishing with fluorescent reds or yellows. With sinking lines I find, whether it be accident or design, that usually the faster they sink, the darker the line, which cannot be a bad thing.

As usual, the best advice comes last. Having spent a lot of money on these lines, look after them and treat them like babies. When you get home, run them off the spool into a sink of tepid water with the tiniest spot of detergent or washing up liquid, wipe with a wet flannel to clean, then dry thoroughly. In season wind back onto the spool; at the end of the season clean, wipe, dry, strip into a shoebox or similar and store in a cool dry dark place. Occasionally during the season, about once a month, give a very light treatment with Permaplas as per directions, for it must be wiped off after treatment. This is a replasticising agent and will keep your line in perfect order. I've got a couple of lines that I still use, seven years old, still in very good condition.

The one thing you must not do is leave your line in a place where it can be subjected to excessive heat, i.e. the car boot, a very warm cupboard or, as I have occasionally seen, the shelf in the back window of a car.

Allow me to suggest a double taper 444 Cortland Floater. It's expensive but looked after will perform better than any other line I know. It grieves me not to be able to recommend a British made line but I haven't had one yet that comes anywhere near in quality, and furthermore it seems to have the advantage of staying supple even in the sometimes bitter cold water of early season fishing. This is a quality not many other lines seem to have.

If you do have this problem of the line hardening in cold water, when it's difficult to retrieve in a small coil in the hand, a good treatment with the Permaplas will do the trick – but don't be too liberal with it. You naturally can overdo this and have the line handle like a soft rag.

Leaders

To me it is going to be simple to tell you what you should buy to make the bulk of the leaders you will need for fishing. My method is simply a spool of 6lb nylon, and it need not be of an expensive brand either for I have found the best of the lot is usually of the cheaper varieties. I prefer a pale green colour.

The thing to look for is a nylon that is not too supple, because a bit of stiffness in it will save quite a lot of grief, but this is just my opinion. Over the season you will use quite a lot of it and, if you change your method as often as I do, you might go through three or four hundred yards in a season. It is cheap enough but the thing that amuses me most is so few anglers understand it. I have often seen another chap fishing and on looking at his leader I am astonished to see that he will have two or three wind knots in it quite happily knowing they are there. Now all these so-called wind knots are just an ordinary overhand knot that I suggest you tie in the new nylon you've just bought. Put the knotted line on a spring balance and see how much poundage you will get before it breaks. I will guarantee that the 6lb line will break much nearer to 2lb than you would imagine.

The moment you detect a wind knot, if it's loose, pick it out with the point of the hook or needle. If you can't get it out, tie a new section in the leader. It takes very few moments to rectify and, if I believe everything I hear from people around me at times, it's always the bigger fish that break them. The simple fact is that even a small stockie will make a leader part under these conditions.

When you take the length of nylon off the spool, have you noticed that when you cut or let go of the end, it springs back into coils, giving you the message that it's got a memory. You can understand the reason why people usually get a tangle soon after tying a new leader, especially in the average lengths I am going to tell you to make. So the first thing I do after stripping enough nylon off the spool to the length I need is to stretch it till it is straight. If you don't, you can imagine what happens on the false casting you must do to lengthen the line to a fishable range. On each false cast at the extreme ends, back and front, you can imagine this piece of nylon trying to spring back together like a corkscrew. So be warned.

All that's needed to make a length of nylon into a leader are two knots, one end tied to the line, the other holding the fly to it and in the act of doing this, you have weakened the leader considerably, for any knot in nylon, if not tied correctly and with extreme care, will create a weak link in the most vulnerable part of your tackle.

Any knot in nylon when it is doubled must be kept at an even loop, especially as it is being tightened, and it must be moistened to prevent any friction, as the heat generated if pulled tight when dry will most surely weaken it. If, when you have pulled the knot tight, there is a loose strand or loop in, it is very suspect. My suggestion is to cut and retie, it's the only sure way. As far as making up a leader is concerned, I only use two types of knot when actually making the leader. The one I use to attach the leader to the butt piece on the fly line is a double overhand loop and the one used to tie the droppers on is the four turn water knot or, as it has been named, the Cove Knot.

So at the moment we have three knots, the loop and two droppers and in tying on the flies, we now have six. The most reliable knot to tie the flies on with is the tucked half blood. Practise these knots till they are perfect, they never let me down.

The only time I use a tapered leader is when I use a dry fly or a single very small nymph. My reason for saying that a tapered leader is unnecessary with a team of flies is that one can balance or unbalance it by the weight and positions you choose for the flies. An example is this – if I chose to put a very light fly on the point, a slightly heavier one on

Fig 2   **The Four Turn Water Knot or Cove Knot**
This knot is for making up a leader with droppers, or joining
pieces of nylon of different breaking strains (for a tapered
leader). It is very important to ensure that both the loops are
of even diameter in order to avoid snapping off.

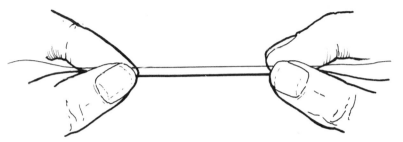

Two lengths of nylon are held
together with an 8in overlap.

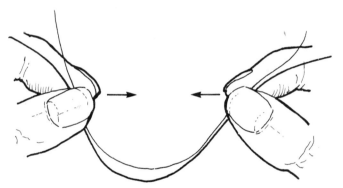

Hold the lengths firmly between the
forefinger and thumb of each hand.

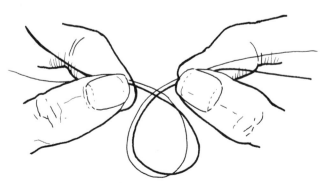

The ends are held close together
and overlapped.

Fig 2 continued

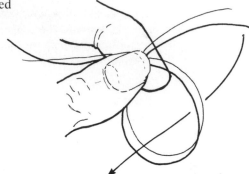

The first of four turns.

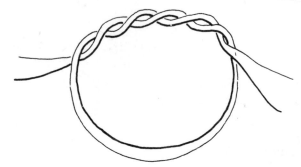

The runs are moistened and drawn
together; the end pointing up the
cast can be left as a dropper. Flies
tied on these droppers will not twist
around the main leader.

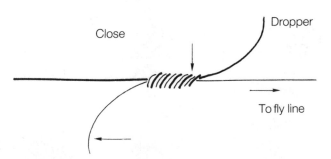

Close

Dropper

To fly line

the first dropper and the heaviest fly on the top dropper, I would be in trouble immediately, but if I reversed the flies, everything would be alright.

So remember when you make up any leader, it's not anything within reason to do with size, *it's the weight that matters.*

Another point I would like to make is that the droppers on this leader should be kept short. When I tie them they finish up about two to three inches long once the fly is tied. This usually stops the tendency of the droppers to wrap themselves around the main leader and so cause more trouble. I have used leaders up to 30ft long with this method with level 6lb nylon and have never felt any discomfort at all. In fact the longer the leader, the less trouble they are once you get used to them.

I remember a chap telling me once after seeing me fish at Grafham, of trying to buy a long leader at Hardy's of Pall Mall and having the assistant tell him that it was impossible for anybody to use a leader that long. The longest one you could get even with droppers at this time was a mere 9ft. It took the manufacturers three or four years to produce a tapered leader of 15ft. They seem very slow on the uptake.

Now finally there are a few basic rules to use to get the best efficiency out of long leaders, and my average leader is 18ft. With a leader like this, put your first dropper 6ft from the point fly and your top dropper 2 to 2½ft from the butt piece on the line. If you increase the length by 2 to 4ft push the first dropper up to 8ft and the top dropper is left in the same position as before, not forgetting to keep the droppers short and making certain to put the heaviest fly on the point and the lightest on the top dropper.

When you move to another pitch with this long leader, wind in till the top dropper joins in the top ring. Get hold of the point fly, taking the leader around the outside of the cage of the reel and put the point fly in the ring most convenient up the rod to keep everything taut. Watch out for the loose dropper, it sometimes finishes up near your hand. If so, do as I do, stick it lightly in the cork handle.

FINE LINES

I know during difficult times, that a lot of anglers feel they would do far better if they went to a finer leader. We possibly expect too much from our tackle and we wonder why we get smashed occasionally when trying to get maximum distance by using a more powerful rod and heavier line. It's no wonder to me that we do for I once experimented, with a friend, trying to find how fast we could go in a boat and still catch fish. We had a light fibreglass craft with a forty horse-power motor; my companion stripping a lure in the wake as fast as he could, still caught fish. I don't know for certain what speed we got on that particular day, but it must have been in excess of thirty knots, and I have read somewhere that rainbows are capable of doing 60mph from a static start.

It is my opinion that when you use powerful tackle and small flies, the weight of the line tends to tear the smaller hooks out; especially if the fish manages to run and put even more pressure on it. This is due to the fact that the more line you have out, the heavier it becomes. The chances of landing fish under these conditions become even worse. It became apparent to me a long time ago, when using my first shooting heads at Eyebrook, that some sort of shock absorber would be beneficial and I tried using a rubber band between the end of the line and top of the leader. Now as far as it goes, this might sound like good sense, but the trouble I found was that the rubber connection stretched and never stopped stretching, so that it was impossible to set the hook hard into the mouth. After losing a number of fish, I gave it up as a bad job but at least the leader never broke and I still kept possession of my flies. I came to the conclusion that one did not need to go to finer nylon to get fish in any conditions on any reservoir. I am very often asked how is it possible to go down to size fourteens with a 6lb leader and I can say with honesty that it has never made the slightest difference to me. Some waters specify the breaking strain of leader to be used. At Chew Valley they advised 7lb breaking strain which, in the circumstances, was sensible. For even in the early days at Blagdon we read that, owing to the size of the fish in there, a lot of the regular clientele used salmon tackle with small salmon flies. When Grafham started I remember one individual, a notable angler, turning up with a double handed rod but for a number of years, I gave little thought to the problems of line weight and elasticity.

But a couple of years ago, I saw Don Neish fitting up tackles for a roach pole and told him of my experiments with rubber. He showed me a new product which is called Optima Power Gum and, upon inspection, I found that, unlike rubber, this nylon based material stretched only so far and that once it had about doubled its length, it stopped and was rigid. I decided to give it a trial and the first opportunity I had was at the Walton Hall fishery that weekend. After needle knotting about 2½ft at the end of my line I put a 2lb leader on and started fishing. I found that it turned over in casting much neater than the rubber ever did and my first fish on it was a 3lb rainbow which, when I got it on a short line, I held hard just to see what would happen. As much as that fish pulled, he couldn't break me, for all the Optima Power Gum did was to stretch to its limit and then retract the moment the strain relaxed and, owing to the gum having such a limited amount of stretch, I kept it under control very easily while not being conscious of it being there. I personally use it very rarely but always have a spool of it in my kit and think it may be useful to anglers who fish the much clearer waters down south, where they tell me you have to go to finer leaders to get fish. Optima Power Gum needle knots neatly and the loop to leader attachment should be made quite large, a loop three inches long is about right, and I would renew it about once a month to be on the safe side. So, if you are constantly bothered by smash takes, take my tip and give it a go.

Fitting Tackle

I think the time has come now for me to explain how I fit my tackle up for use:

The first thing you must do is to tie a knot in the end of your backing. Put the reel on the rod, feed the backing knot through the butt ring and round the spool, tie a running noose, pull it tight up to the spool and wind it all on, leaving three or four feet loose. Get a strong needle and unpick the end of the braided backing, half an inch from the end, and leave.

Exposed braided   Whipped with
inner core   a bobbin

Strip the dressing from the core for about 1½in. Unpick the braid for ¼in. Turn back to form loop and bind tightly with fine rod binding thread. Varnish with a flexible finish e.g. Vycoat.

Fig 3 **Whipping the loop for a shooting head**
     The smaller the loop, the better the line will travel through
     the rod rings. Nylon backing is tied to this loop with a
     Tucked Half Blood Knot (*see* Fig 8).

Now take the fly line and unwind it onto the floor, taking care not to tread on it. Take hold of the end you are going to join to the backing and, with a cigarette lighter, very quickly melt the plastic coat at the end of the line (it doesn't take much heat) and with your thumb nail or a blunt knife, clean it off until the braided centre is exposed. Tease this out till the strands are straight. Now you're nearly ready to whip them together. If you tie your own flies, get the bobbin out with your whipping silk attached (the heaviest one you've got). If it isn't heavy, attach a piece of lead to it and put it on the table, then cut yourself a piece of nylon, 6lb, about six inches long and put it on a table where you can see it.

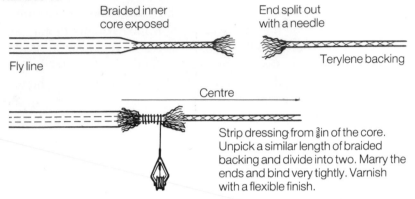

Fig 4   **Whipping fly line to Terylene backing**
The neatest way of attaching Terylene backing to a fly line.
Small and neat, it will run through the rod rings perfectly.

Now pick up the end of backing from the reel and divide the loose strands into a V, roughly equal, and do the same with the stripped end of the fly line. Push one V into the other and hold between finger and thumb. They should overlap so that the total length is just about the half inch. Now picking up the bobbin, trap the tying silk between the same finger and thumb that are holding the line together. Start to spin the bobbin round and round, back over the loose ends of the tying silk until you trap it with itself. One good tip is to keep the distance between the bobbin and lines reasonably short, say about four to five inches, otherwise you will sock yourself under the chin. Take your time going back and forwards along the braid until you have a nice neat tapered join. When you are satisfied, pick up the piece of nylon which I have usually brushed off the table by now, and double it. Lay it alongside the braid and proceed to spin for another half dozen turns, making a whip finish by cutting the tying silk, pushing it through the loop in the nylon and by pulling the two loose ends together, completing the join. Cut off the loose end, then varnish with a flexible finish two or three times. Leave to dry. When dry, wind it onto the reel, leaving five or six feet of the fly line loose.

Now get a piece of nylon, preferably the butt piece from a knotless tapered leader, about six feet long, tapering down to about 12lb to 10lb

Fig 5 The Needle Knot

The use of the Needle Knot for attaching line to butt piece will ensure a smooth flow of line through the tip ring.

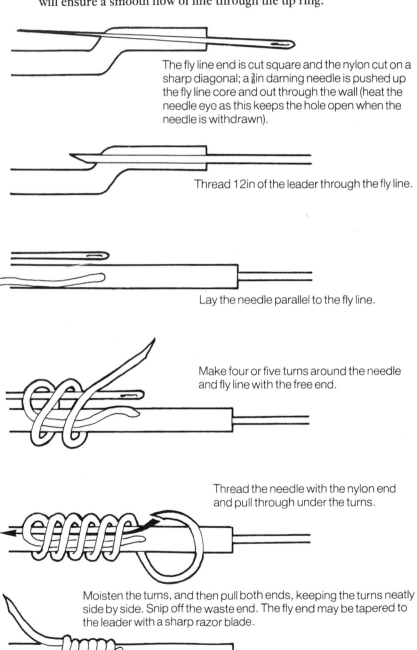

The fly line end is cut square and the nylon cut on a sharp diagonal; a ⅜in darning needle is pushed up the fly line core and out through the wall (heat the needle eye as this keeps the hole open when the needle is withdrawn).

Thread 12in of the leader through the fly line.

Lay the needle parallel to the fly line.

Make four or five turns around the needle and fly line with the free end.

Thread the needle with the nylon end and pull through under the turns.

Moisten the turns, and then pull both ends, keeping the turns neatly side by side. Snip off the waste end. The fly end may be tapered to the leader with a sharp razor blade.

breaking strain (I cannot understand why somebody doesn't produce them). If unavailable, a level 15lb will do and needle knot to the point of the fly line. I find that when the needle knot is completed, it pays to trim the surplus to a stub of about ⅛in long and after it settles down within a few hours' fishing, it should then be retrimmed flush to the knot.

Fig 6   **The Improved Needle Knot**
This only works with tapeworm, but its use offers even less trouble than the standard Needle Knot. It is more difficult to tie, but worth the extra effort.

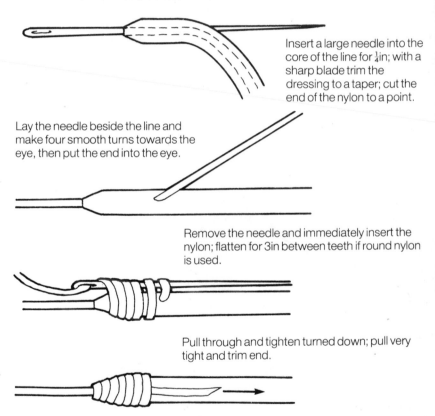

Insert a large needle into the core of the line for ¼in; with a sharp blade trim the dressing to a taper; cut the end of the nylon to a point.

Lay the needle beside the line and make four smooth turns towards the eye, then put the end into the eye.

Remove the needle and immediately insert the nylon; flatten for 3in between teeth if round nylon is used.

Pull through and tighten turned down; pull very tight and trim end.

Then tie a large double overhand loop in the end. I say large, three to four inches long, because I find that if it is made small, it doesn't pull alongside itself, causing drag problems. This is the loop that attaches it to the leader. All knots should be trimmed short and neat and the butt piece, in all probability, will finish up about three to three and a half inches long. Done in this way, the butt piece will, if looked after, last a complete season.

Fig 7   Double Overhand Loop Knot
The longer loop will cause far less wake than the middle one because it tucks tógether better.

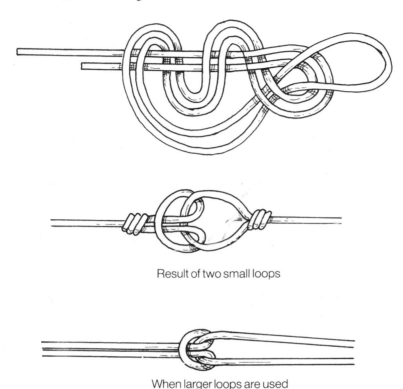

Result of two small loops

When larger loops are used

While we are still on knots, I find that most people don't complete the tucked half blood knot correctly when attaching the flies to the leader, so study the sketch closely. Mostly it is because they do not complete the final tuck and often they are left with a little piece of curled nylon at the end of their leader. I cannot stress this point too much. Take extreme care with every knot. One weak link and a leader is useless.

Now if you haven't got another reel, use a spare spool and make it up with another line exactly the same. The reason will become clear later.

I use another reel and put on an old double taper that has about come to the end of its useful life, usually cracked but not with any of the surface plastic missing. This makes a total of three. Two good lines, one rough line. This is my complete outfit that I carry with me in my bag, apart from rods, reels, leader materials in cloth bags, fly boxes, one

Fig 8 Tying a Tucked Half Blood Knot
The safest knot for attaching fly to leader. Note the final tuck.

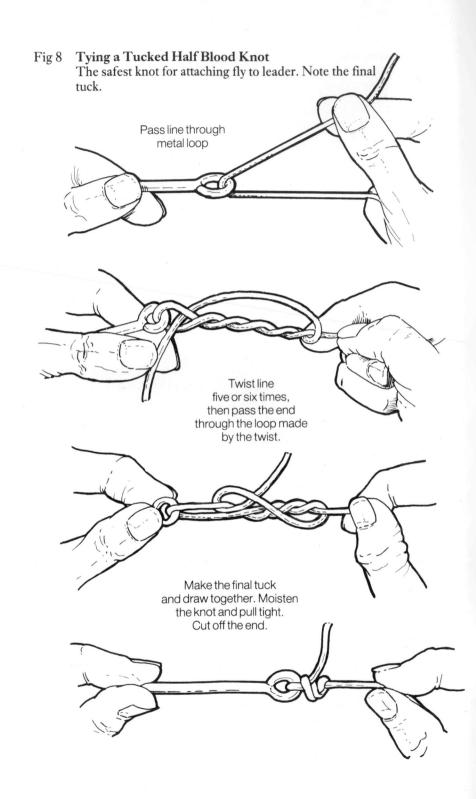

Pass line through
metal loop

Twist line
five or six times,
then pass the end
through the loop made
by the twist.

Make the final tuck
and draw together. Moisten
the knot and pull tight.
Cut off the end.

large reserve box, one small empty box pocket size, one priest, one marrow spoon, box with needles, spare tip ring and butt ring, roll of plastic adhesive tape, spare lighter flints and a spare bobbin. Once, forgetting my reel after cleaning it and not putting it in the bag before I went to work in London, I had to buy one down there, complete with backing and a new line. My practice in those days was to get down in the early evening, nip up the A1 and get a couple of hours in at Grafham before I headed home. On arriving at the water, I put the backing on the reel but had no bobbin to whip the fly line to it. So I tied it on by putting a knot in the end of both braid and fly line, wound it on and proceeded to fish. After having a few normal fish, I turned back to see a great big boil about twenty yards in front of me which I quickly covered with a size eight Pheasant Tail. The fish 'took' instantly and pulled the rest of the fly line off the reel until the knot between line and backing went through the butt ring and jammed against the next ring up. The fish of course, not liking this much (I cannot say I was overjoyed either), shot upwards, stood on its tail and I remember thinking to myself 'about six pounds' and deciding I had to do something about it. Keeping the rod tip high, I started to back out of the water and knocked the sense out of him in about a minute flat. On beaching him, the bloke nearest me walked along and said 'What a nice fish, it's about eight pounds.' I said 'No, it's about six.' So after getting his spring balance, he came back and weighed it. 'Seven and a quarter' he said, adding 'I've heard about you and how rough you treat fish. You get them on the bank quick don't you?' My reply was 'Oh yes, it's amazing how quick you can knock the stuffing out of them.' But I dared not tell him that I had no choice, owing to that ruddy great knot I had at the time. So I never travel now without that bobbin.

The one thing I will advise is the advantage of wearing a good fishing waistcoat. All that I need for a session's fishing can be kept in the pockets and after sorting out the small amount of tackle, flies etc which I need about my person, I usually leave the rest in the car and use that as base.

CASTING

In general I have very little to add on this subject because I think very nearly every individual seems to develop his own style. One or two things I will mention are that practice generally makes perfect and I still do it. Concentrate on a good presentation and, with care, you can catch a lot of fish at short and medium ranges, but it does at times pay to be able to put a long line out.

Keep the cast back as high as possible; let the line straighten before coming in to the forward stroke.

My final word of advice is that an hour spent with a competent professional will save a lot of hard work. Once you have had the mechanics of casting explained to you, I don't think you will go wrong. Oh yes, be prepared to pay. If you wanted to become proficient at any other sport you would expect to do this, and it's money well spent.

WADING

If possible, don't. I've found in the last ten years or so that a lot of times it's unnecessary and I managed to cure myself finally by going fishing mainly in low shoes and, after getting wet feet quite a few times, gradually gave it up, although the wet feet were far more welcome than the wet crutch, legs and feet I used to get.

I sometimes wear thigh boots or even calf length now, purely as an aid to keeping dry under wet weather conditions and not as a means of pushing the fish further away from myself and other anglers. I tend to use cover and camouflage and if there's room, try to fish the quiet places.

CLOTHING

The warm, dry, comfortable angler is the one most likely to get fish. There is nothing worse than being cold and miserable with rain running down the back of your neck. I know, I've had some of it. Nowadays I always put plenty on, on the principle I can take it off if I get too hot. Use good quality waterproof jackets and leggings, a good hat, and I usually take strips of old towelling to stop water dripping down my neck.

FLY TYING

One of the greatest joys in fly fishing is taking fish on flies you have created yourself and I always consider that the purgatory I went through was well worth it. It always amazes me how rough a tying I can get away with, especially with the nymph creations. I am a great lover too of traditional flies and endeavour to tie them in the old style. Some of them have been taking fish for centuries and while they still kill, who are we to try to beat them. I sometimes think that this is one branch of the art that is deteriorating if the samples I see of some of them on sale are anything to go by.

There are, however, Fly Dressers' Guilds around the country that do have very good instructors at very little cost and I would advise anyone interested to get in touch with them. I know, many people who join them are tying very good creations in quite a short time. May their tying silk never break. I will myself often use wet flies with nymphs and at times find them more than useful. Once again, thanks to the instructors at the Grafham courses, from whom I received many tips and hints – John Veniard, Donald Downs, 'Taff' Price and others. Those sessions used to go on well into the small hours and I know all the people on the staff were really knackered at the finish of these weekend courses, especially me.

I remember one session that carried on till about 2.45am on a Sunday morning and, going home to get some more flies, sitting in the chair and falling asleep. When I woke up at about 7.30am, I jumped in the car, wanting a few fish for autopsy for my class. I thought to myself that this had to be a rush job because my lecture was due to start at 9.00am. I dashed down to the water in a certain little bay, tackling up by 8.15, and quickly got in between two anglers already there. I asked one how it was going and was told 'very slow'. He had caught one fish that had taken as soon as he had started and had seen nothing since.

First chuck produced a brownie 3½lb, next a rainbow 2½lb. I missed one next chuck, but two more chucks produced a couple of stockfish about a pound apiece. I picked up the catch and shouting 'Cheerio', dashed off up to the car park and arrived at the centre dead on time.

Well, I said it was a rush job! There was a sequel to this story – that night, speaking to one of the bailiffs in the boozer at Perry, he told me that a couple of anglers had told him of a poacher coming down to the same bay that morning. He had four quick fish and dashed off, and they were sure he didn't have a ticket. No, I didn't let on it was me.

2 Early Season

A Large Midland Water in April

Now I'll take you fishing. Imagine it's April. It's cold as it usually is at this time, the wind is blowing with clouds scudding across the sky with a hint of rain showers to come. Not a very cheerful backdrop to a day out. However, we've decided to make a start. Put the tackle in the car, making sure we've got a couple of hot flasks and plenty of warm sweaters and good waterproofs and waders (at least to keep our legs warm even if we aren't going to wade). We make a quick check that everything we'll need is on board as I once, in a rush, forgot my rod! It's 10.00am, time to get moving.

On arriving at the lodge, we buy our tickets and, if we are new to the water, we read the fishery rules, which in some cases is like reading a novel – I wish more fisheries would simplify them. The best waters usually have very few.

However, I know this place well and will put you straight as we go along. Normally if I were a stranger to a water, I would take the time and trouble to do what I call my homework by obtaining maps that give contours and depths and if they are big waters, I try to make friends with the surveyors and try to get their plans showing the top water levels of the area. Moreover, a few hours spent with the locals in the nearest hostelry will reveal quite a lot of useful things and, even if they don't fish, farmers, farm workers and gamekeepers are a valuable source of information.

The main features which I find useful to know are matters of local geography: where the feeder streams enter ditches; where are the dykes, old ponds, quarries, stonework walls, steep drop offs from the bank, and so on. It's amazing what one can learn in a very short time, especially where roads and lanes ran through before the land was flooded. Roads and lanes normally have ditches running alongside them, and it is also essential to work out your access to certain points around the water. Remember not to park in gateways or block exits and access to other anglers' vehicles and farm machinery. Most landowners are very tolerant if approached in the right manner. 'What's all this got to do with fishing?' you may well ask. I will answer 'A hell of a lot,' and

When tackling up, make sure the knots are perfect; if not, you will be in trouble right from the start. Retie anything that does not look right.

will impress upon you the fact that I know that a lot of quick entries to good water have been cut off because some thoughtless twit has parked in a place that has caused great inconvenience to local people. We are their guests, and even though at most times we have to pay for the privilege, good public relations do no harm at all. Better by far to keep things on a friendly basis.

As I pull down a lane into a farmyard the lady of the place comes out and I wish her 'Good morning'. Asking if it is still OK to park my car in the lane further down, she says that's fine and we do so. A polite word and a couple of fish occasionally work wonders and it's saved us a mile and a half's difficult walking, and not only that. The chances are that, being a fair old distance from the nearest official car park, we won't be contending with the crowds that, in most instances, are not prepared to walk for the privilege of peace and quiet.

Getting out of the car, we put on warm clothing, waders, over-trousers etc. On making up our rods, you ask what reel to put on and I tell you, 'Just the ordinary floater' which we put onto the butt straight away. I tell you we'll make up our leader down at the water and you pick up all your tackle and flasks and grub. Then I ask what you want that lot for. All I have is my rod and reel in one hand. I've got a spool of nylon in my waistcoat. I have also transferred a couple of dozen flies from my big box into the small one and now have it in my pocket, together with a film case full of sinking compound made with some clay I got earlier, mixed with a little detergent, a tin of grease in another pocket, more due to habit than in the hope of using it on a day like this. After making you shed most of your unnecessary items, I lead the way down to the water with rod in one hand and flask in the other. I take you round a slight rise to a sheltered bay with a breeze blowing slightly left to right down the feeder stream which runs into it.

You say 'How nice it looks.' I remark that I didn't pick it for its looks – I picked it because it's sheltered, because it's two overcoats warmer than standing on that exposed bank, because I know it usually holds a lot of fish and most of all because it's quiet. The only other anglers we can see are a long way across on the other bank, most of them in groups talking to one another and no doubt thoroughly cold. Although I know that some of them have probably got a few fish, it's not my scene at this time of year under these conditions.

I tell you to make up a leader 18ft long, putting the first dropper 6ft up from the point and top dropper 2½ft from the butt piece, reminding you at the same time to stretch the leader to remove those coils where it's been on the spool. Having done this, I tell you to put a size eight

Pheasant Tail on the point, a size ten Black Spider on first dropper and a size twelve Black Spider on top, the Spiders being the ones with the minimum of hackle to ensure that they will get down a bit.

While we are doing this you say that you haven't seen a fish move yet. I tell you that you may see one or two later but that it's very unlikely at this time of year as it's far colder than you think; we're very sheltered in here. As I put some sinking compound on the whole length of the leader and butt piece, I tell you to do the same. It gives you the advantage that as soon as your flies touch the water, they're fishing for you and, although I wouldn't expect a trout to rise at this time, I have had it happen and hope springs eternal.

We stand about thirty yards apart, trying a few casts across the bay, rippled slightly by the wind out of the valley where the feeder stream meanders. I tell you, as I lift into my first slow draw, that you are not allowing the flies to sink deep enough before you start to retrieve, and this one took while the tail fly was virtually scraping the bottom. In fact I thought the draw was my fly stuck in the weed, but I always lift on these occasions. Anyway, 'nothing ventured, nothing gained' is my remark as I slide a nice little rainbow of about 1lb ashore. You say that it didn't fight very much and I tell you that they don't when the water is this cold and that they will be totally different fish in a month or two's time when the water warms up. All of a sudden you give a whoop of delight as a fish splashes on the top and your rod bends over in a nice curve. Seeing it's about the same size as mine, I tell you to keep the rod well up and ease it up the little beach of silt. You stand to admire it and I tell you to get your flies back into the water quickly because these rainbows usually travel in a shoal and you might pick up a few of them before they go swim about. A cast later you are into another which, unlike the other fish, has taken the Black Spider on the first dropper which I tell you is quite usual as most of the chironomids that hatch in early season are the black variety in any case.

I then see a slight putter in the ripple, slightly to the left of me and putting it down lightly, 10ft or so upwind of it, start a retrieve to intercept it. Then, with a splash and splutter, it takes the top dropper and I explain, as I pull it aground, that if one sees a fish move and can put a fly quickly in its path, one usually gets an instant reaction. I laughingly add that any fish that comes up in this weather is looking for trouble and this one certainly found it.

Occasionally, even when fishing slow and deep, it pays to do a much faster retrieve because sometimes an odd fish will take at the surface and it can relieve the monotony of the deep slow grind and concentration of fishing deep. I then further explain that if you are fishing normally and a fish moves at the surface within range, you should lift off your line in the opposite direction you want it to go as you will find it very difficult to bend the fly line in the air. If you do it right, you can generally put it in the fish's path with just one lift and delivery, not emphasising too much that I said into the fish's path, for I well remember an article written by a well-known scribe, pointing out that reservoir anglers were the most inaccurate casters of the lot. I disagreed instantly, saying that most of the anglers I fly fished near usually hit them on the head, very often with the end of the line. This results in the fish, with a massive swirl, disappearing towards the horizon at very great speed. Remember the fact that most fish feeding at the surface are travelling against the wind and drift.

It's been quiet now for the last half hour and you say you don't think you are getting deep enough. I know your spot, which has the old brook line closer in than where I am. I take my fly box out and produce a size eight longshank Stick Fly, the caddis imitation, and tell you to put it on the point in place of the Pheasant Tail. A few minutes later you are into an obviously better fish which, although doing nothing violent, certainly puts a curve like a longbow at full stretch into your rod. Well, I'm just as happy watching as fishing and so I move along to see as you slide a big black rainbow of about 4lb into the shallows. After wetting my hands, I manage to unhook it without damage and hold it upright in the water. I convince you that it's inedible and that it will be worth your while to let it go because it will probably recover and be a nice bright fish in a month or two's time. You nod approvingly and I let it swim off. I can see the disappointment on your face and I try to cheer you up by saying that there are a lot of good fish in this bay and that the chances are good as it's tending to brighten up a bit. I suggest we have a cup of tea so we put our rods down resting upright against a bush, so that if anyone does walk along they will not damage them, and you ask me if it's possible to avoid these out-of-condition fish.

First I point out that the chances are there are a fair few black or out-of-condition fish in the area. This is because the feeder stream is in close proximity and I take you up the mouth of it and show you scores of them, all shapes and sizes, actually nosing the stream and some going quite a way up it. Some of them are hen fish and a lesser number are cocks, up to 6lb. These are the real dark fish with patches of white disease showing on some of them and we also see a few dead fish which appear to have been struck at by herons. I point out that, although we are fishing at closest some forty yards from the mouth of the brook, no doubt a lot of spawn minded fish are drawn into it because the flow of the stream keeps to its original course and carries into the lake a fair way. Indeed, I have had times when the wind has been blowing directly into it, when my line has actually been pulled against the wind by its force. Of the five fish we've landed at present, only one has been a 'black'n' and I find that with a smooth slow retrieve, they give me very little trouble. However if you were fishing a sunk line with lures or impart a much jerkier retrieve, even with small offerings, you would get most of them.

A particularly rough black fish.

This leaves me to explain that it is against this fishery's rules to return fish and I wonder what the reaction would be in a court, seeing that the law is so strictly defined against the taking of gravid fish? I sometimes think that, especially in the case of the larger waters, it would be a better policy to net them out where possible and keep them in tanks or ponds until they recover or die. Nobody in their right minds wants them. It's the larger reservoirs that get this problem most, owing no doubt to the water taking a lot longer to warm up.

Great! The sun has now come out again, so let's get back to the job in hand. On getting back to my tackle, I change the point fly, and put on a tiny Jersey Hand and instantly pull out three fish, one a nice brown trout of 2½lb in very good nick. Sometimes even these can be lean at this time of the year and I tell you to come up closer to me and give you the same fly. For I know that under these bright and gin clear conditions it will take fish, and often you will see the fish following into 2ft of water to take them as you lift your rod up slowly. Now we catch fish steadily until the clouds cover up the weak sunlight and we revert back to the Stick Fly on point and finish up with seven fish apiece, some of them up to the 2lb mark with the exception of the one brownie. We've had enough anyway, it's 3.30pm and we walk slowly up to the car and, as we pass the farm, I stop to give the lady a couple of fish. On the way home I tell you a story about the same spot in nearly similar circumstances some years ago which went thus.

It is very often safer to beach a fish. Larger fish in particular often cause a commotion when they see the net, and then break off.

A young fellow came to me and asked me if I would teach him to catch trout. I offered to take him on the following Sunday, telling him that I liked to go home for lunch and if he wanted to carry on, I would return at 2.00pm or thereabouts. Well, I took him and we arrived in the bay and much in the same style of fishing, I soon had eight fish on the bank, all about a pound to a pound and a half. I left him about 1.00pm, and being early in the season, I gave him two Black Lures and told him to use them if he got desperate.

On my return about 2.30pm, the weather had brightened up considerably, and I found him with waterproof jacket off, flogging out as far as he could. He turned round and came out of the water and told me that as soon as I had disappeared up the hill, the sun had come out and he had seen a few fish moving out as far as he could cast. He had decided to put on one of those 'black things' and had thrown it out and one of them had taken it right away. 'I had a hell of a job getting it out, so I took that Black Lure off and put the other one on and slung that out and another one took it.'

I asked him what was the problem and why had he changed the first lure. 'Ah well,' he said 'it wouldn't float and after I got the second one, I had a hell of a job drying them off.' Lifting up his coat from the ground, he then revealed four beautiful rainbows between 3 and 3½lb, bright as new pins. At that time, the average fish for that water was about 1¼lb.

Well I more or less told you we would have a few fish but most of these were taken by feeling the fish pull on the line and I'll take you out again in a month's time and show you another easy way to get fish with nymphs if the weather conditions keep true to form. It wasn't just luck you see that we were more or less in the right place using the right flies with the right methods. A lot of our success was due to good homework and watching the weather and wind direction.

The landing nets we didn't take 'on purpose'. I do not use a net in places where they are unnecessary. Knowing it was a gently sloping bank, I knew we could beach them quite safely. More are lost at the last moment when the fish is pulled into very shallow water and has a bloody great shape standing over it, poking it in front with this net. No wonder they're terrified. I am very often standing 30ft back when beaching a fish. As long as you keep plenty of life in them, even very big fish will beach themselves as long as you keep their heads pointing bankwards. I don't think it's possible for them to reverse! The tackle used was the normal floating line which I explained was a slight sink tip with an 18ft leader with first dropper 6ft above point and top dropper 2½ft from the butt piece.

Flies used as tail fly or point were Pheasant Tail or Stick Fly until the sun came out, then a small Jersey Herd fished nymph fashion – dead slow. First dropper was a size ten Black Spider with a sparse hackle and the top dropper was a size twelve Black Spider dressed with sparse hackle.

The method of fishing was mainly allowing the tail fly to sink to the bottom or very near and retrieving in a coil to hand very slow and smooth. Occasionally we did a faster retrieve to fish all three in the upper surface by not allowing any time to let the point fly sink very deep.

We had a great advantage through picking the right situation. I knew it would be reasonably calm and it offered an opportunity, if the wind did change, to move to the other side of the bay in shelter again. I also knew that this water, although freshly stocked, held a good head of over wintered fish. I knew that the depth was about 10 to 12ft deep within casting range and I picked the best time of day. Under these conditions, I knew that there would be no serious drift factor caused by the wind, which we would have got had we fished from the open bank. And we had no disturbance from other anglers.

A Second Day

It's 10.00am and we're at the lodge once again and, owing to someone opening their big mouth, we can't go to that nice quiet bay. It's now crowded and they're probably slaughtering those black fish in the brook mouth. Never mind, I've got another string to my bow and we'll go completely in the opposite direction. Owing to the amount of walking we are now going to do, it's very unlikely we'll be disturbed much again today. But let this be a lesson to you – if you find a good spot, keep it quiet until you have finished with it. Most of these early season hot spots have a limited duration owing to pressure from fish-hungry anglers waking up from hibernation.

The weather and wind conditions are much about the same and we get back into the car, proceed round the reservoir and park. We travel light with the same tackle as last time. I know the spot we're fishing, so I add a few more flies from the main box and off we go, through the gate, up the brook, over the bridge and back down the other side, getting over the fence, jumping a couple of ditches and striding out as best we can through the old dead undergrowth, round willow trees and bushes. Sounds like a commando course doesn't it – feels like it too. Another half mile and we come across a shallow part of the reservoir which I know dried out last October when the water dropped to its lowest level. Although we can see tufts of grass sticking out of the water in places, plus the odd willow clump, most of the water we will be fishing over will be from 4 to 6ft deep, plenty deep enough to cover some good fish. As they seem to put more fish in when stocking at this end of the lake, they sometimes (the stockies that is) seem to pull a fair few better fish with them.

There is nothing like a few stockfish to liven up the resident population. I'm almost sure that when these are dashing about, the bigger fish think they're missing something and gather round to see what is going on. If this does happen, I'll show you how to miss these sprats and get a few better fish.

It's a little more exposed here, with a heavy wave from left to right, but we are alright, because the wave isn't colouring up the water; possibly because the silt is being held together by the roots of the grass and weeds that usually grow right the way across when it is dry.

I tell you to make up a leader the same length as before, 18ft long, first dropper 6ft from point, top dropper 2½ft from butt piece. You say that that sounds long for fishing water which I reckon is 4 to 6ft deep, but I assure you that I doubt if you will touch bottom at all, owing to the amount of drift. I can see that the lee shore is about three-quarters of a mile upwind of us, and that this will allow a fair amount of drift to build up, especially in this shallow water. The only thing you will catch apart from fish, I tell you, will be an occasional bit of dead grass. Now taking my fly box out of my pocket, I give you three Black Spiders and tell you to put the size twelve on the top dropper and the size ten on the middle and *this* size ten on point. You can't see why I am so specific and say that these size tens are the same. I instantly tell you to take a closer look, remarking that I thought I was the one with bad close up vision. Of course you now see that the hackle of the point fly is pattern No.3, the one with the most hackle, which I am using because I want everything to fish shallow. I also point out, looking at the water, that there's the odd little black fly on the weed already and I've seen a couple of fish move.

OK. So you cannot understand how the larvae (which I have told you is in the form of a bloodworm of different colours, not all red as most people suppose) survive when the water goes down and the lake bed is completely dry. I tell you there is plenty of moisture to keep them alive under that baked coat that remains on top. I read somewhere that there are probably some 400 different types of chironomid and believe me, if you don't see these same or other types in a barrel of water left out for a few weeks in the back yard, there's something wrong with the water. I once spent a very long time looking into water butts. 'Charming' you say, and I say 'Let's get on with it, mud up your leader.'

You try casting across wind and let it swing along with it for a few yards and then start a slow retrieve. I watch you closely as I know by the fish I've seen responding to the hatch, that they will soon be at you, and on the third chuck, a fish splashes about where your flies are. You lift and touch one but miss it and I tell you that with all that belly in the line which has blown down wind before you started to retrieve, it pays to keep the rod low and move it from right to left against the drift, making the line slide across the water towards you. This is all you need to do to get a good hook hold and by lifting the rod you are giving the fish slack line. You toss out again and as the line swings, you do everything right and you are into number one and play it to shore very quickly. A nice little stockie about 1lb. Well, it's a start anyway. You knock it on the head and a couple of casts later, you get another and remind me that I said I would show you how to miss these sprats. No pleasing some people, is there? I tell you you've got to have guts to miss the stockies. The next time you get a take, ignore it and let the flies come out of its mouth because the fish will surely spit them out. Then throw the bit of line upwind to cause the bow in it to go slack. This allows them to go slightly deeper where these better fish often sit. Sometimes the line will slide solidly away, and usually they're the better fish. The stockies take with more of a quick snatch. You try this but after ignoring the first take, the stockie is still there. Shame it hooked itself but try again. You can't win them all. And in the next cast, after ignoring the first snatch, you are into a better fish, a nice rainbow of a couple of pounds.

Well, you are four up and I haven't made a start yet, so let's have a cup of tea in the shelter of these bushes and I'll tell you a story.

When I lived over at Exton close to Rutland, I used to dash up the A1 to get at least a couple of hours' fishing before dark and one evening, managed to get down to Whitwell Bay by about 7.30pm. It was crowded because it was blowing a gale from the Normanton side and the bay was the only sheltered place to go. I stood watching a line of anglers pulling out stockfish one after another and a good friend of mine, Claud, who used to own the Noel Arms at Whitwell, said 'Come on in between us two, there's room for a little one like you.' This was an offer I could hardly refuse, there being not really enough time to go round to the other bank, seeing it was going to get dark by about 9.00pm or soon after.

So I tackled up with the usual long leader and a couple of Blacks on the droppers and a size eight Pheasant Tail on point, muddied my leader and chucked out. Now I must explain that Whitwell Creek, the one on which the fishing lodge stands, is very deep. The moment the flies hit the water, I had an instant little boil and a snatch which I ignored and let the old Pheasant Tail continue on its way down. Sure enough, the line slid slowly away. I lifted, and after an exciting but quick struggle, I beached a rainbow of 4lb. Meanwhile, my neighbours got a stockie apiece. Straightening out my leader, I recast and did the same with the next cast. I ignored the quick snatch and waited till the line went solidly away – this time a 3lb fish. I think I had done this seven times when Claud said to me 'I just can't understand it, every time a blinking coconut.' Of course I told him what I was doing, got my number eight and was away by 8.30pm. All I can add is that Whitwell held a hell of a lot of big fish. Come on then, let's get to it.

I try a few casts and it's not long before I'm into a fish, and repeat this till I get my whack. As I start to take my flies off, you get your last fish also and it's not yet 3.00pm. By the time we get back to the car, it's 3.45pm and you say 'Hooray for the little Blacks' and I tell you that we were lucky really as sometimes that particular situation doesn't work out quite as well and that if I don't get a fish within the first hour, I usually start hunting. Well we *were* fishing in a jungle anyway. I've found over a period that it works out that I get generally four decent fish and four stockies in this area at this time of year, and I don't complain. We've managed the average again today on the nymph team I call Faith, Hope and Charity.

On the way home I start to tell you about the Black Spider patterns, how they evolved from the complicated chironomid patterns I used to tie way back in the early days at Eyebrook through to Pitsford, Chew Valley, Blagdon and then Grafham, only to learn that most of us had been too clever by half, and how I came to learn that the simple little Spider beat the lot of them in all situations. I had it in my box all that time, but that's another story.

'How many times did you get caught in the rubbish?' I ask finally, and am pleased when you tell me that it only happened a couple of times. That cross drift can be very strong, and remember that the fish will feed all day, or at any time of the day when conditions are right during April and May. This is usually when the water really starts to warm up, and the most difficult conditions you will find at this time of the year are the bright cold days when the wind is coming out of the sun. At these times, fish deep and slow with something bright on point, even a Corixa which, with a white body and silver rib, can shine like a jewel in water.

3 The Change in May

You can fish the previous two situations with the utmost confidence while the water stays cold. The water under normal conditions will probably warm up slowly and you will, if observant, notice life start to appear in and around the water's edge. But the one thing that will be most obvious to you some time (depending on weather conditions) between the end of April and the middle of May on most waters, is a massive hatch of usually dark coloured chironomids. You will notice this gnat like insect that sometimes swarms on the skyline and also at times spirals into the sky as far as the eye can see. These insects often hatch out over the very deep water and fly ashore first to rest and then swarm and mate. Then the female insects fly back to the water to lay their eggs to complete the cycle. Now you may have noticed that I mentioned the 'usually dark coloured' chironomids and take it from me, at this time of year, they are dark coloured. If you make a really close inspection of them under a magnifier, you will see that they vary a fair lot in actual shades from black to very pale green, even to pale red. But at this time, the Black Spider usually kills fish the best. It's really no problem knowing what imitation to use and at certain times during a day's fishing I'm tempted to say that you must be prepared to change your presentation from minute to minute. However let me correct myself to say 'from cast to cast' for I am a great believer in the fact that the more versatile an angler becomes, the quicker he'll fill his bag.

Let us once again imagine a typical situation. I'm at the water's edge. There's a nice gentle ripple going from left to right and as I walked down from the car park I noticed the swarms of insects flying around and resting in the grass, bushes and trees. I haven't put my flies on my leader and I never do until I have looked at the water and weighed up the situation. With all these clues, I really can't go wrong and experience tells me as I put the three Black Spiders on and muddy the leader, that the fish will very likely, being opportunist like me, be feeding at a lot of different levels during this session. My leader is the usual 18ft and on the point is a size ten wide gape hook on the heavier wire hook, on the middle a size twelve, and on top dropper, a featherweight size twelve. As I muddy the leader with a piece of blue clay from the bankside I mould the remainder into a ball about ½in round and press

Nine times out of ten you will want to fish below the surface.
Muddying the leader means that the moment the flies go below the
surface, they are fishing.

it against the rod where the cork joins the blank at the top of the handle. Having done this, I tap my waterproof jacket pockets to make sure I've got a tin of Permagrease in each, my fishing waistcoat being under the jacket.

I begin with a tentative cast, straight out in front of me and, because I have seen nothing close to me, let it settle before I start retrieving, allowing the fly on point to sink as deep as it will.

Don't get the impression that just because I have an 18ft leader on, I am getting down to a depth of 18ft. For with this gentle ripple and ultra slow retrieve, I know that I am probably getting down six or seven feet, at most. But I know that the pitch I am fishing, even at my most extreme casting range, is not above 12ft deep at this stage of the proceedings. This is important for me to know and as you can visualise, it slopes gently from ankle deep at the bank, deepening as it goes out further. I also know that trout when feeding at the bottom with an abundance of food available, will only move a certain distance to intercept an offering and if it's too far away, it's just not worth their effort to come and get it, in more ways than one.

I continue exploring the water, casting fanwise, even very close to the bank at times, retrieving a little faster when I do this to stop my tail fly fouling the bottom.

All of a sudden I notice a movement about thirty yards downwind of me and, although I have at that moment only retrieved about half the line I had out, I instantly drop the coil of line in my left hand and strip the rest in, quickly lifting my rod up to catch the leader in my hand. At the same moment, I reach in my pocket for the tin of grease. Now there are tins and tins as you will appreciate, and before I put them in my pocket I always make sure that the lid comes off easily. Now having transferred the leader I am holding in my left hand with my rod trapped under my right arm, I quickly put three dabs of grease on the leader, one about a foot above the tail fly, one about a foot below the first dropper and one a foot above the first dropper. Then I put the leader in the water in front of me. I proceed to lengthen line in front of a small shoal of fish which have proceeded upwind to nearly in front of me, about twenty yards out. I deliver the flies about 10ft in front of them and as I expected, one accelerates and grabs the fly nearest to it. I lift and it's on.

Now read back and go through the sequence step by step. It's a ploy which gets me a lot of fish.

First I observed the movement of the fish. Second I knew full well that they would be coming along upwind towards me. Logic says that, as I had not seen them going downwind, they must be moving up, and

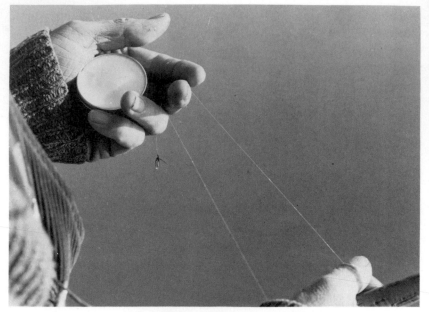

Greasing the leader. When fish are feeding on the surface, a tin of
grease can mean the difference between success and failure.

under most instances fish at the surface travel upwind. Third, I knew I
had plenty of time to pull my line in and grease the leader. Fourth,
when I saw that it was a shoal of fish, the chances were, owing to the
'dog in a manger' attitude that very often prevails with shoals of fish,
that if I put my flies close enough on an interception course, that one or
two would dash at them. Fifth, I had the 'guts' to stand still and do
nothing and let the fish hang itself before I lifted the rod to drive the
hook home. If I had moved the flies I might have caused a bit of wake
that could have put the fish off at the last moment. I do believe that
when you put grease to a leader it pays, more often than not, not to
retrieve at all and let wind and wave do the moving for you.

OK you may say. I might have got that fish without putting grease on
the leader and by casting immediately in front of them and commenc-
ing to retrieve instantly to keep the flies high up in the water. After all
there are only four ways that I know of keeping flies up at the surface or
near to it and these are by greasing the leader or fly, using a dry fly, or by
using one of these ultra modern type tyings with balls of styrafoam in
the dressing, which by the way I don't find very successful, or finally by
speed of retrieve. You take your pick but I find grease by far the most

If you cause wake like this, you're in trouble. It's the surest way of frightening fish away. To avoid wake, either muddy the leader or retrieve more slowly (or not at all).

rewarding way.

Don't hang about when you've landed it either for the chances are that you can get back to the water quick and pick another one or two out of the same shoal. If no one was fishing upwind of me, I would probably do a quick shuffle up to intercept the same fish again and again.

Let's imagine though that I get back to fishing and after a few casts get no more results. I am letting the flies drift round close to the surface and retrieving slowly when they drift round to an angle where I am forced to retrieve reasonably close to the bank. If the wind is strong, you can, with a little practice, learn how to 'mend line' to stop the leader and flies drifting round too fast. By throwing the back end of the line upwind it can make a lot of difference. But I get no takes and so get my blob of mud off the cork, muddy the leader again and go back to fishing slow and allowing the fly on point to go deep. With this method combined with the occasional greasing, and fishing normally, I will most likely limit out fairly quickly. Versatility is a bloody good fisherman, I'm with him often!

I forgot to mention, I dropped the tin of grease back into my pocket after dropping the leader onto the water.

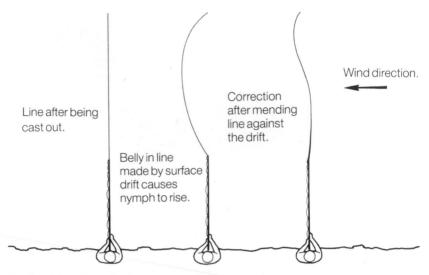

Line after being
cast out.

Belly in line
made by surface
drift causes
nymph to rise.

Correction
after mending
line against
the drift.

Wind direction.

Fig 9   **Mending the line**

The Change in May II

The flat calm, to most fishermen I meet, is the *dreaded* flat calm and it
always amuses me that so few of them know how to deal with it. I can
honestly say I would much rather fish a flat, even from a boat, which
most anglers think is worse still.

And to master it in my opinion is a matter of compromise for, as you
most likely know, under the climatic conditions that cause them to
appear (centre of col I think the weathermen call it), you must be
prepared to sacrifice a lot of distance in your casting to get a perfect
presentation. If you try to force your line out to the length that you can
achieve under normal conditions, you will find it hard, no, very hard, to
put it down nice and straight with a minimum of disturbance. I will
stress here and now that this is the last thing that you will want. So now
we will get out the reel with that old line on it that I told you about. Rig it
up with a leader of about 14ft, putting the droppers at the same
distances as before. Now comes the hard bit – you have got to find some
nice clay. If you are in some parts of the country I know it's impossible,
so use a sinking compound of fuller's earth and detergent, and you'll
need plenty of it. I prefer the clay. Pull your line through the rod rings
and start to muddy the line with it, all of twenty yards. Sounds drastic
doesn't it? I can see rod manufacturers throwing their arms up to
heaven and either thinking of the complaints that their customers are

likely to send in owing to rod rings wearing out in a very short time or doing handstands thinking of the new rods they'll sell when you do, but I can assure you neither will happen. As I told you before, it's lasted me on one rod I've had over ten years and there's lots of things you can do which will ruin rod rings faster than this. As for the line, it's an old one and, if yours are like mine, at the end of its useful life as a floater anyway. Once you have done this initial muddying, tie on your flies for a start and muddy the leader as well, then try a cast or two and see if you can retrieve it, both slow and fast, without causing a wake with any part of it. You may have to spend a half hour sometimes muddying repeatedly to get it fishing right but as you will find, it will be time well spent.

Now back to the natural history for a bit. Under flat calms the pupae of these chironomids usually find it very difficult to pierce the surface tension caused by the calm. I imagine most other insects that hatch from the water have the same problem. Hence these periods are not the time when you see very good hatches in any case. But usually there are quite enough insects about (probably they hatched earlier) returning to the water. And then there are those that are trying to hatch anyway. So you will usually see the odd fish rising in quite a few places, purely because you can't miss seeing them.

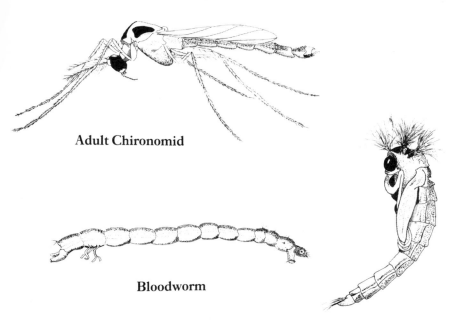

Adult Chironomid

Bloodworm

Chironomid Pupa

The most difficult thing you will find is trying to master where to put your flies down, even if you see fish rising quite close. For these fish usually move around haphazardly, mopping up the food as they go and there is no pattern at all to their track. Sometimes you will see a single fish ringing the water over a period of a minute or two and if it is well within range, it can be 'tried' by putting the line down well in front of where you think it is likely to be showing next. Notice I have not recommended that you retrieve straight away, for the real trick is to stand still and do absolutely nothing until it moves again, hopefully within about 10ft of where your flies are. It no longer amazes me under this situation, how far a fish will move to attack your offering and how fast they swallow it. I always wonder why they do it, for under these conditions the things they are really feeding on are, to my eyes, mainly static.

The best example I can give of an actual fishing situation is this one. Fishing with a friend at Grafham on one of these so-called dog days I managed to nobble a pitch on a point, my mate having arrived about half an hour later. On getting down to me, he asked how I was doing and I told him that I had a couple and I was soon going to have another, having seen a fish 'ring' once about twenty yards to my right and about the same distance out. It showed again about a half minute later, some fifteen yards to my right, the same distance out again. I lifted my line from the shallows and laid it out in anticipation that the fish would keep on the same track. A few seconds after I had done this, it showed again about five yards to the right and chancing my luck, I still did nothing. Then it showed with another little ring, two feet from where my flies lay in wait. I gave two short sharp pulls on the line and on the second pull it was there, and I remember as I slid it ashore, my friend said 'You waited for that', and went round the corner into the bay. I landed this fish because I managed to get a position where I was likely to be able to intercept fish that I knew usually come across this particular point from another one about two hundred yards away on my right, and also because I observed, over a long period of time, that most never ventured into the bay under these conditions. I knew for a fact that the bay itself always held a lot of fish in any case, but that they rarely revealed their presence at the surface at these times.

You might make the assumption, probably rightly so, that I was chancing my arm by waiting so long and that if I had started to pull when it was that five yards from my leader, it would have had a go anyway. Yes, but in this case, it was a matter of taking out 'insurance'. For I knew that, if I could get the fish very close to my leader, I could get what I call a 'reaction take'. I explain it like this; if you can get a fly close enough to a fish without disturbance or leave it until the fish is in very close proximity and then move it suddenly, the fish reacts automatically and attacks it. I fully appreciate that trout are not machines, but nine times out of ten this works, and that particular fish was an easy one for me because at least its path was fairly predictable, which I have said before is rare in a flat.

Now with a couple of points to clear up, we will leave this situation for a much better one.

Why didn't the flies sink down when I waited for the fish to get close to my leader? Well, they're not very heavy in any case and I suppose the surface tension must have something to do with slowing down the rate of descent, the same thing with the line which *must* be by design just under the surface. Now I know you will think that a slow sinking line would be the better thing to use, but I can assure you now that although it will catch a few fish, it's not so certain to be where you want it if you have to wait for a fish a long time. That old floating line with your help is a valuable part of your repertoire. Many people say (when seeing me in action), that they haven't got an old line. I usually ask them if they want a good line at the end of the season or a freezer full of fish.

Another thing I suppose I ought to mention is that, although it may seem that there is absolutely no wind, you must do a few trial casts to different points of the compass. I have no doubt that you, like me, will find that there will be one direction in which both line and leader straighten out far better and find a pitch to take advantage of this. I can't emphasise too much that to give the best results, both line and leader must land soft and straight.

Sooner or later, if you have not got your limit, you may get lucky and if you are having problems getting results, a front comes through and a breeze starts blowing. It blows into the bank where you are located. So many times I have seen other anglers pick up their gear, go up to the car park, jump in their cars and drive to the other side of the reservoir to get this wind at their backs. If they only knew what they were missing! The first indications are feeling this wind on your face and looking across the water. You see a ripple advancing across the lake towards you which pushes all the flat towards you, and as this continues, it pushes all the floating dead, dying and hatching insects in front of it. The trout will now advance with it until they are usually at very close range, sometimes at your feet. This oily-type water can remain on this now downwind shore for some time, up to two hours, and I suppose it's like some fishy banqueting table laid out with easy pickings.

Casting to a rise. If Arthur Cove sees a fish rise, he casts into ripples on the edge so that the fish doesn't notice the leader.

Well, one ten yard cast into a multitude of fish is better than a hundred yards into barren water, and if you keep your flies up on the surface, retrieving by moving the flies slightly faster than the inward drift, you should be well rewarded. But be warned, the responses can be violent as the fish usually turn upwind when they take.

There is one final act to this chironomidal saga which involves the female insect coming back to the water to lay her eggs, and to me it's probably the most satisfying period of all. This action can happen in early season at any time of the day when the water and weather conditions are right. For the average angler, the problem is recognising when this happens. Usually the guide is that it occurs from lunchtime till late evening, until about the end of June, and after this till the end of the season from early evening till dark. These events can be very localised, especially on the bigger waters.

The real trouble in these cases is that you can be twenty yards away from the right pitch and nothing you can do will have any effect. All the activity will probably be in front of your neighbour and if he does not know what is happening, he generally does no good either. Like you, he will have a few fish by sheer persistence but will be refused by nearly every fish he puts in front of. Now the signs to look for are the female chironomids returning to the water. Sometimes this is not very obvious and it's more likely that you will see that intense activity of the trout taking at the surface and by their very brisk movement, be lulled into thinking that they are fry feeding. The boils and turbulence that they make in this type of rise can be most misleading. I know from bitter experience that if this turns out to be the case, it leads to a lot of frustration and at such times, have seen good anglers go through their fly boxes and throw their rods down in desperation. Of course there is an answer and I am reasonably sure that it has very little to do with the pattern of fly you are using. When you open your eyes and see how these little blighters actually go about regenerating their species, you will begin to understand. And after studying them, I can tell you that, as in most cases of mastering difficult fish feeding at the surface, the answer is in the type of retrieve you use or lack of it.

If you watch the female chironomids you will notice that they will skim across the surface against the wind and drift in spurts. They stop, I presume, to lay a few eggs and skim forward again and repeat the process until they are spent. Sometimes the action stops on the edge of the ripple and, if you are in a pitch where you can put your flies well into it, the take comes usually right on the dividing line between this and the flat water. Occasionally, if the whole area you are fishing is flat, you have to be just a little more careful with your deliveries into the area of activity. If you 'line' a fish or two, wait a few minutes before you start the retrieve which should be in long steady pulls from the butt ring to down to your side. These are pulls of 2 to 4ft long and the stop is usually when one has pulled down to the side. The lapse is between another grip on the line as far forward as you can go towards the butt ring. Now the real secret, if you don't want to get smashed too many times, is to pull the line between finger and thumb of the rod hand and at the same time not gripping the line too tight in the left hand. If you get what is usually a violent tug at any time during the pull or stop, you can let the line slide between your fingers and so eliminate the chances of a break. Now just think to yourself, a long pull and a stop, a long pull and a stop.

I think the female chironomid knows more about drift in a lake than we are ever likely to know and I think that why they skim against the drift is possibly because they know that the eggs will sink to the bottom. Thus they are likely to be scattered over the deep water rather than be washed up on the bank. The mayfly, in the same way, always flies

Hand lining. The long pull and stop is the classic buzzer retrieve. It is a useful tactic to use at times when the female chironomid is coming back to the water to lay her eggs.

upstream to lay her eggs in the fast streams because maybe nature tells her that if she did not, they would have all finished up in the sea millions of years ago, thereby cancelling out the drift downstream as she hatched.

Ideally, I would say that the best rig for the job would be, if in ripple, the normal floater; if in a flat calm, the muddied up line and three black flies – the Spiders are preferred. But if this happens in your pitch at any time, don't dash out to change your flies, for if you have anything on of a reasonable size, be it a size eight Pheasant Tail to a size ten Mallard End Claret, they will still take the fish as long as the retrieve is right.

It's a good job for our sake that most trout can't be that bright. You may well ask me, after telling you that a particular female skims across the top laying her eggs, why I don't use a dry fly, something like a dry Black Gnat. Well I have and you will find, as I have, that not many dry flies will stay on the surface very long after you have pulled them through the water time after time in a session. As long as you keep your nymph team somewhere close to the top, I'm sure the trout won't know the difference. If they did, possibly they would not take them so readily. Furthermore I will point out that this rise to the so-called Buzzer has nothing to do with the preoccupied rises you will meet later in the season, of which more later.

Late May to Early June

In a normal season, the water usually starts to warm up quite rapidly from now on, and another sequence begins.

I am talking of the time when the scum which has sunk to the bottom begins to reappear. Formed by rotting weed, algae and so on it starts to appear at the surface again. This is probably caused by gaseous action triggered off by warming water and once again, my method depends on the weather at the time. Now you will probably notice somewhere round about this time of year, if it is a flat calm, when you commence to fish, that the water is covered with scum. You cannot get your flies and leader to sink below, and if you stand and watch for some time, you will notice these chunks coming up to the surface. They can be all shapes and sizes and sometimes cause a boil as they appear. A lot of anglers when they see these chunks decide not to carry on as it is unfishable. 'It's that thick you can't get your flies through it,' is the most used phrase.

Now this is the time of year I love the most. First of all I know that summer is really starting to arrive and I know that the fish are likely to

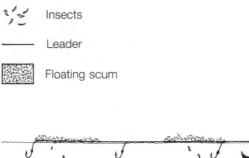

Fig 10   **Taking advantage of floating scum**
Insects which are prematurely lifted to the surface by rafts
of rising scum drop back to the bottom to continue their
life cycle.

be feeding all day. You can imagine all the goodies that have taken
residence in this stuff lying on the bottom – the snails, nymphs,
shrimps, bloodworms – you name it, fish will eat it. All of a sudden
these animals are lifted from the bottom to the surface and don't like it
one bit at all. They jump off these rafts to dive back to the bottom again
and, once again, the trout, seeming to know this one, are cruising
underneath these rafts, waiting for them. This is one of the most
profitable times to get good quality fish with very little effort at all.

Now in the flat calm, the best way to approach the problem is with a
normal floating line with an 18ft leader and with any normal selection
of nymphs. I can suggest a size eight Pheasant Tail on point, a size ten
Corixa on first dropper and a Black Spider on top dropper. There are
many combinations which you will find profitable; including Black and
Peacock Spiders, shrimp imitations, bloodworm patterns and any
beetle patterns you may have. The choices are legion but nearly all are
effective when cast across this scum. Just hold and wait as usual. Probably the first indication will be a boil and a pull from the fish, for what
usually happens in practice is that the nymphs will have penetrated the
scum, and being supported by it along the length of the leader, are in
exactly the right position where the trout are waiting or cruising below
for this exodus back to the deep.

You can of course give the leader a tweak or two occasionally and, if and when your leader goes through it, as it occasionally will do, make a slow retrieve, keeping the flies fishing below it until you are either fortunate or have to lift off to repeat. If you see the odd fish moving in the area you are in for a whale of a time.

Now sometimes it can happen that when there is a good ripple or a wave on the water, this scum tends to get sucked into the calm lanes between the rough water and this will give the flies all the movement you need, and of course once again your fellow anglers will be complaining about all the rubbish floating around.

Try to pick yourself a pitch where the wave or ripple is running alongside you, that is along the bank in easy casting distance of the lanes where you will see the scum clearly. This is the time when you will see the odd fish move at the surface or boil and you will no doubt sometimes be surprised how close they will come in. Cast your leader slightly upwind across the scum lanes which, depending on the strength of the wind, are sometimes from a foot wide to four feet across. Let the whole lot progress downwind at the mercy of aforementioned wind and wave and one thing I will bet on, if the fish are about, you will not wait long. I love to let fish hook themselves, so wait till the fish pulls your rod, tap round and then do the rest. If you do not get a response, repeat after the flies have drifted close in downwind of you, but I doubt if they will get that far. Usually the action is fast and furious – a most exciting way to fish. This situation can sometimes last a fortnight or so if you are really fortunate, so make hay while the sun shines, so to speak.

THE BLOODWORM OR 'RED DIDDY'

I cannot finish this part without mentioning the larval form of most of the chironomids. This is the bloodworm, and take it from me, they are not all red. Like the adults they vary a lot in colour from very pale, nearly transparent, to greens and deep red to crimson. The first time I really noticed them was in the early days at Eyebrook but I didn't appreciate their true value until about two years after Grafham opened.

Things were getting quite difficult for most anglers there, for after the flush of the first half season and the start of the second one, it suddenly started to be a different ball game. But by inspecting the stomach contents of every trout, I realised that bloodworms were beginning to feature more and more in the diet of the better fish. So, I decided one day to try to make a passable imitation of this great big bloodworm (and I had found quite a few up to 1½in long).

I started by tying dark red silk ribbed with yellow onto a longshank size eight hook, varnished it, tried it and had a few fish on it. But after further observation of them alive in the water, I noticed that although they lashed about a lot in the water, they never made any real progress of travel through it and, like most of the other non-swimming nymphs, they were really at the mercy of wind and drift. I tied them with longer tails to try to improve this lashing action without much real movement through the water. Well, to cut a long story short, after trying hackle feathers sticking out behind pieces of silk, wool cloth, leather (you name it I tried it), they usually finished up with the tail wrapped round the body. I wondered what I could do to get it right and eventually came up with an articulated worm consisting of joining one hook behind another with a piece of nylon and when completed, nipping off the bend of the rear hook. They were a bit more successful and caught fish but still didn't have the real action I needed. It was a conversation with a good fishing mate, Eric Bridgeman of Wollaston in Northamptonshire that gave me the good idea of using a rubber band – red of course. Using the natural bend in them, I could make the tail curve back over the shank of the hook.

I tried this in the bath (my usual testing tank) and, realising it was still immobile, I decided to shave the piece of rubber down closest to the shank where it appeared from under the crimson silk I used for the body. Eventually I got it to kick with a very slight tweak from the nylon I had it tied on. Success at last! The shaving down of these rubber bands was nearly as exciting as catching fish for, as you can imagine, I had to shave them real fine in the one particular spot and I would often ruin half a dozen before getting it right.

Well, I tied up a dozen of these crimson bloodworms and on the Sunday went to Grafham with Rodney. We were fishing in a line of anglers in the Yacht Club bay, not doing a great deal, so decided to try one of these latest creations. I banged it out a couple of tweaks on nice slow draw and I was into a good fish, repeated in the next three casts with the same result. Rodney, not backward in coming forward, was soon tying one on and in his next cast he was into a fish and the word went right along the line of anglers, each in turn coming to me and asking for one of those things we were catching on. They all without exception caught their whack.

The one thing I did find out over the next few weeks was that the few of them that attempted to tie copies hadn't twigged that the most important part of the pattern was shaving the rubber band down real fine. The next time I went fishing with Rodney, the first thing he asked for was one of those 'Red Diddy' things. That's how it got its name.

Well, things got to such a point over the next couple of months that it was only a matter of putting the Red Diddy in the water and fish stuck themselves on it, and some funny things used to be said about it. I remember one evening after dashing up from London on my way home, calling in at the lodge before I decided where to go for the last hour or so. I appeared by the side of the lodge and heard one of the bailiffs shout to a chap down below the veranda, 'Here's a bloke who'll have his limit before he goes home.' This bloke answered that he'd fished the last three weeks without catching anything and there weren't any fish left in there. I went up the steps into the lodge and the money was being laid. Before I could get anything on, it had been decided that I would get my limit before dark, it then being 8.30pm. It was going to get dark by 10pm.

I had noticed, when coming along the road, having nipped into Gaynes Cove car park, that there were five anglers in the narrow part of the cove and decided that this was the spot to go. With the wind blowing out of it, it usually pulled fish down from the dam and when they got into the shallow water near the mouth of the brook, they turned round and came back out again. So if you were in the narrow part, you could get two goes at them – if they didn't take on the way in, you got them on the way out (lovely theory isn't it?).

On going down, I was pleased to see that the man in the spot I always thought was best, the pitch nearest the fence, was packing up and I got into that spot. Eight casts, eight fish and I was back in the lodge in an hour and nearly home before dusk. At that time, the bay was full of bloodworm and that was that. I never got a penny out of it – not even a drink.

To tell you the truth, I got fed up with the bloody thing (get it?) and after doing unholy slaughter with it over the following season, I could even go out in a boat when fish were really hard to find, toss it over the side and it wasn't many minutes before my line was being stretched. I stopped using it and have never tied another since. One little sequel to this story is that some years later I was given some of the spiralled nylon tube and was asked to give it a try. I put a length of it on a size ten hook, leaving a tail about ½in out of the back. I put a small Grey Head on it, went round the west bank, saw a fish move about twenty-five yards out and tossed it out to it. The next instant the fish was on – a rainbow of 3lb. Two casts later I was into another 2½lb trout, so cut it off and ground it into the mud, thinking to myself, this is where I came in.

BACK SWIMMERS AND CORIXA

When you look at the little creatures around the shallow sides of most ponds and lakes in the British Isles, one of the first things you will notice on the bare mud and silt and among the debris on the bottom are some little insects that look like small bugs. They creep about the bottom usually in fast jerky movements and come up to the surface, usually in similar movements and sometimes they spiral back to the bottom. On closer inspection, they can usually be defined as shore bugs, back swimmers, and the one that fascinates me, the water boatman or *corixidae*, the Corixa as we call it. It's one of the deadliest patterns you can have in your box, or better still on your leader.

I honestly don't know how many variations there are, but I know that there are at least a couple of dozen and that they vary a lot in size and colour. The largest I have seen was ½in (and possibly one nearly 1in which I saw in Church Hill Farm fishery but didn't catch so I haven't got the proof). However, the average size is smaller than ½in down to tiny things. They are beetles, and the back which has wing covers, is like a hard shell that splits down the middle. At times they take to the wing and can fly quite fast.

One thing I have noticed is that they tend to live in colonies of different races and at the larger waters such as Chew Valley, Pitsford, Grafham and Rutland in certain bays and ditches, the varieties are distinct in body colour and size. In Gaynes Cove at Grafham I found a type that had a distinctly yellowish coloured body while on the other bank in Savages Creek, they had a whitish coloured body and were much larger. As usual, it pays to observe and experiment to suit your own locality for the colour range is great, from a dark grey, to brown, olive green and so on.

The most usual size I tie them are on twelves and tens and I tie them distinctly low water fashion – the dressing finishing two-thirds along the shank of the hook. This may appear peculiar and possibly might look as if there is too much iron showing, but it doesn't make any difference to the fish and it does ensure that you get a good hook hold. I also tie a few on size eights and occasionally get fish on them. I am a great believer in using a reasonable size hook for often this pattern works best in rubbish filled ditches and close in to the bankside weed where one must hold fish hard to have any chance of beating them. It pays to stalk the shallows standing well back from the water for I have found it to be the most profitable pattern around the sides really close in.

In the early days at Chew Valley, it nearly got me into trouble with the bailiffs. One Sunday, once again fishing a steep sided ditch, keeping well back from the edge, I was dragging fish out as usual. I never saw another soul get a fish and, believe me, there were enough there. All of a sudden I was tapped on the back and a fellow asked me what I was up to. I turned round, recognised one of the staff and told him I was educating his fish. He asked to see my flies, and I told him not to snatch them out. My line still in the water, I handed him the rod and told him to lift it up dead slow himself which he did and sure enough, as he did a brownie about 2½lb took the Corixa on the point, putting a violent bend in the rod. I left him to it and walked to my bag a dozen yards away and poured myself a cup of tea. When he had landed the fish and closely inspected the three Corixas I had on the leader, he came over to me and asked what sort of flies they were. After I had explained to him what they imitated he told me that a certain person had driven over to the lodge and reported me for maggot fishing. I told him that as I spent a lot of time watching my line for takes, it didn't leave much time to look over my shoulder for bailiffs and I didn't need to do that anyway. He apologised for troubling me and about an hour later, another old fellow came down to apologise for reporting me. I gave him a few Corixas and showed him how to use them and we became quite good friends over the next few years. I always appreciated the fact he came to me and told me that he had reported me and was man enough to admit he was wrong. I have never cheated in any way while fishing. I'm a hungry hunter and don't need to.

There is one fishery where I rarely fish without a Corixa on the leader and that is Ringstead Grange in Northamptonshire. I've had rainbows up to 11lb on it and two salmon as well.

It's really most deadly in the ditches which usually run into most of the big reservoirs, and sometimes in the most awkward places it pays to fish it with a single fly on an 8lb leader – in those spots where there are very often brambles and blackthorn under the water. Once you hook a good fish, you have to hold them really hard to keep them out of the snags and once again I must warn you of the size of the fish you will find in such places.

SHRIMPS

This is one of the most neglected imitations in reservoir angling because they are superabundant in most waters, including fast running rivers and streams, and are a readily available source of food to fish of any description. I do not know how many varieties there are but I imagine that there are several. I guess they must go through a period of change during their lives for there are quite a lot of differences in size and colour from nearly translucent to orange. I say orange very deliberately because I observed the orange coloured shrimp many years ago at Grafham and in a much larger quantity at Rutland Water and was decried much at one time for suggesting such a thing. The one thing that was obvious to me was that the locality of this coloured shrimp was never in its natural habitat, i.e. close to the bottom or in the bankside weed beds under stones. It was always swimming at the top, sometimes even at the surface over very deep water. Very strange indeed, and it's quite plain to me that in its vulnerable position it soon fell prey to marauding trout. I tied quite a few patterns in this colour and very deadly they were too. I saw quite a few at Rutland again after this time and continued to catch fish on the imitation. Then, while fishing in Eire at the beautiful River Erriff in Galway, a river completely controlled by the Central Fisheries Board, I followed my usual practice of fishing hard all day and sitting up talking all night with the Board's resident biologist. On this occasion struck I 'gold' not orange.

Knowing we were having a day on Lough Tanyard, the lake at the head of the Erriff river system, primarily for sea trout, he asked me if we would kill all we got as he was studying their feeding habits in the lough. Being most interested, I asked him the diet he had found in their stomachs. He told me that they generally included *Gammarus pulex*, our shrimp. When I asked him if he had ever come across an orange variety, he nearly fell off his chair and told me that I was the first angler he had met who had come across them. It seems that the shrimp acts as a host to a little wormy type creature whose name is a thousand times longer than itself – *Pomphorhynchus laevis*, hence referred to as *P. laevis*, and in simple terms they actually take over the shrimp completely. The shrimp itself is probably in great distress and leaves the bottom and takes to more open water where, without its inbuilt sense of colour and camouflage, it falls victim to any fish in the locality.

He told me that there was a paper written at Exeter University by C.T. Kennedy, P.F. Broughton and P.M. Hine of the Department of Biological Sciences, headed *The Status of Brown and Rainbow Trout as hosts of the Acanthocephalan, Pomphorhynchus laevis*, and that he would obtain a copy and send it on to me, which he did. On receiving the University paper, I found in the first few paragraphs all I wanted to know and quote once more, 'Infected shrimps were recognisable as such by the *orange colour*.' And furthermore, I found out they can live quite a long time with these parasites in them and can move quite fast. And once inside a live trout's stomach they move on to a further stage of

A day's catch of wild brownies. Lough Arrow, Eire.

regeneration. I had noticed in some trout that I had caught at Rutland that the worm had moved into the rib cage of them.

I find that I personally get great co-operation from the scientific staff of the Central Fisheries Board in Ireland and I am indebted to all the people on the old Inland Fisheries Trust and now the Board, for all their help and consideration over the years, and in particular young Martin O'Farrel at the Erriff Fishery, for giving me the answer to the orange shrimp.

You see a lot of us do keep our eyes open and I remember George Wood, the head bailiff at Pitsford, showing me a sedge larva there one day. He was doing some field work for Leicester University, and said 'I bet you haven't seen this one before,' and upon looking at it, saying to him 'I'll tell you where you got it, out of the ditch on the other side of the road from here.' He replied, 'Good God, you don't miss much do you. We think it's a hybrid and it's only found in that place.'

It does pay to be careful and not to jump to conclusions. I remember once standing in the water again at Pitsford and, upon spying a stickleback floating at my feet, I picked it up to have a close look and got quite excited to find that it had five spines. I've studied fish all my life and I knew that this did not exist, at least in British waters (we seem to have the three and eleven spined varieties). Popping it into my bottle and with visions of contacting the British Museum, I got it home, put it under my magnifier to find it was an immature eleven spine with the very tiny extra spines just coming through. I was not too disappointed – the very last thing I want is a stickleback named after me.

Plate 1 Small Black Spiders

This plate shows how the Small Spider may be varied by controlling the number of hackle turns.

1 Two-turn hackle   2 Three-turn hackle   3 Four-turn hackle

Plate 2 Small Spider variants

The Spiders shown here are colour variants of Plate 1. As with the Small Black Spider, the number of hackle turns may be varied.

1 Silver   2 Green & Yellow   3 Brown   4 Claret

Plate 3 **Pheasant Tail Nymphs**

1 Cove's Pheasant Tail Nymph   2 Green PTN   3 Grey PTN
4 Black PTN

Plate 4 **Corixa**

1 Brown   2 Silver   3 Green

Plate 5 **Other flies used by Arthur Cove**

1 Amber Sedge Pupa   2 Green Sedge Pupa   3 Stick Fly
4 Orange Shrimp   5 Orange Seal's Fur Nymph   6 Gold Ribbed
Hare's Ear   7 Green Pea Nymph   8 Pale Green Nymph
9 Jersey Herd Nymph   10 Daddy-long-legs

Plate 6 (above)   1 The Cove PTN   2 Typical shop-bought PTN

Plates 6 and 7 demonstrate the differences that there may be between Arthur Cove's own patterns and commercially tied patterns.

Plate 7 (below)   1 The Cove Orange Seal's Fur Nymph
                  2 Typical shop-bought Orange Seal's Fur Nymph

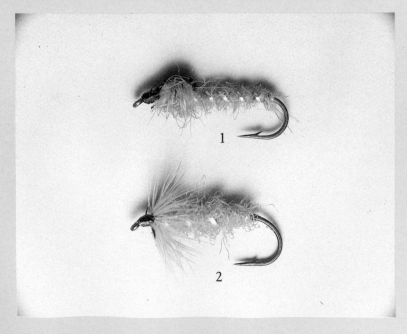

4 June and July

Early June or the Dreaded Curse

Well, all the patterns of flies that I have mentioned up to now have their days, and if you go about your business quietly and efficiently, you should have improved your bag. The next one to rear its ugly head is the caenis hatch or so-called fisherman's curse. But approached in the right way it is not half as bad as is made out.

For the uninitiated, the caenis is the pretty little pale coloured fly that usually starts to hatch about this time in millions and climbs all over you. They shed their skins like snow. Most anglers who fish all day have got their limits by the time the flies appear which is normally towards evening. They will come out earlier, but it's us evening anglers who have to bear the brunt of them.

You may well be tempted to tie intricate little copies of caenis and some of those I have seen are very good indeed. If I could tie them, I would be proud. The whole surface of the water is covered with them and the best hatch usually occurs when there's not a great deal of ripple, and if I said millions, I meant trillions of them. How can one compete with one more pale little fly pitched on the water which will make not a scrap of difference? I know of not one angler who can claim success by matching the hatch once the hordes are present.

And, yes, I have got a for instance too. Many years ago a certain well known professional fly tyer from down south came to visit me and wanted an evening's fishing with me. I took him over to Pitsford and arrived as the old caenis were in full swing.

On tackling up, he came along to me, opened up the palm of his hand and showed me the most delightful tyings of caenis I'd ever seen. I declined his offerings with great thanks, telling him that I never used such things. I tied on a size eight Pheasant Tail on the point and he went away shaking his head in disbelief.

The action of the fish under these circumstances is quite predictable as they cruise just under the surface at an angle of 45 degrees with their mouths just opening and shutting, rapidly gobbling all and sundry down in one continuous feast. They usually come in very close to shore and once again, with very good presentation, you can take your toll of them. This I did, purely by being very accurate and dropping the Pheasant Tail about a foot beyond and in front of the fish and, without pause, on a short line (no more than ten yards) I just lifted the rod so that the nymph skimmed past their noses at a steady smooth rate of knots. One in about four would peel off and swallow it. Well, in a very short time I had eight fish on the bank and I'm very sorry to say my companion never touched one. In the pub later he took his hat off to me with the remark, 'I'd heard a lot about you I didn't believe, but I'll take it all back now. If they tell me you lassoo them on 2lb points they won't hear me complaining.'

I didn't tell him that if the old 'pheasy' hadn't worked, I still had another ace up my sleeve, for sometimes the little Pale Green Nymph listed in the tyings is better.

A little logic goes a long way to filling your bag. I can remember one occasion many years ago, again at Chew Valley, when the whole lake was full of fry from bank to bank. After fishing from first light till about 11.00am without an offer, I looked along the bank to see my mate waving me back to the tackle, indicating he'd just made a brew. Getting back to him and drinking a cup of tea, I found out that he had done no better than I, and nobody he had seen or spoken to had taken a fish either. But he, as I, had seen plenty of fish move as indicated by the fry jumping out of the trout's way, very often with hundreds leaving the water at the same time. I watched him plodding back to the point he was fishing, some way along the bank and sat there finishing the pot, weighing up the situation in my mind and watching the water, still seeing those fry scatter occasionally.

All of a sudden it occurred to me that if I were one of those poor little fry, I'd jump out of the way too if some horrible great trout came close to me, even if he wasn't after me in particular. Well, you must see how my mind was working, putting myself now in the trout's way of thinking. If I had eaten fry in the amount that was possible, for I surely couldn't miss them, I would be fed up in more ways than one too. Going over to my bag, I got out one of my fly boxes, sorted out three of the Green and Yellow Nymphs I had there and tied them on.

I walked quietly over the bank, lengthening line as I went. A surge of fry moved about eighteen yards out, chasing a great big ring. I dropped my nymphs into it and waited and, sure enough, as they slowly sank, the line tightened up and I was into a nice fish of 4¾lb. I managed to get another four by about 2.00pm and in fact the disturbances were getting fewer and fewer. Most of the fish were moving much further out now so I went back to base, got the old stove going and put the kettle on. Seeing as it was a bright sunny day, I'd put my five good fish under a tussock of grass in the shade.

My mate, seeing I'd got the kettle on, came back to me asking how I'd done. I pointed at a great big tail sticking out from under the tussock. He went over and said 'You beauty, sodding hell' as he caught sight of the others (I don't seem to move in very refined circles do I?). 'What did you get 'em on?' Pointing to my rod propped up against my bag, I told him to look. After inspection he looked at me long and hard and said 'What made you put those on?' 'Simple logic.' He said 'You can't be that bloody simple with fish like that.' I tried to explain to him that it was us who assumed that the trout were taking the fry when, in actual fact, all the fry were doing was getting out of the way as the trout came up to feed on nymphs.

Well, as you can guess, he put a team of my Green and Yellows on, went back to his pitch and we both finished up doing well.

Lesson – don't always take for granted what your eyes tell you is right for very often the conclusions are wrong. Sit down and have a good think. A frustrated angler seldom catches fish.

Well, there is a sequel to this story. The following week we went back, taking another young friend with us. We told him the drill and as usual we scattered in different directions, my mate and myself from the previous week having half a dozen fish each by lunch time. Our young friend came back with fourteen nice fish, and when asked if he was doing what we told him, he replied that he found he caught them by dropping it into the disturbance and stripping it back like a lure – he got them faster that way. Well, you can't win 'em all can you?

June and July

This time of the season to me is one of the most exciting times, for conditions seem to change from day to day. Sometimes they go back to a cold week or so, or can change rapidly to what some call flaming June. I look forward to starting to catch fish on the drop.

Perhaps I should explain those few words more fully. The fish now are much more keen, and starting to get strong. When hooked they fight their weight, and are sometimes prepared to come up and take your offerings while you are waiting for them to sink, hence 'taking on the drop'. At various times from now to the end of the season they will react in this way if you are patient with them.

Also at times from now on, you will have to box a little more clever to get the best results and so begin to use the third line that I suggested you make up at the beginning. This floating line will be greased to its full length with Permagrease so that it floats on top of the water, even down to the very tip. At times you will begin to catch fish by sight, watching the very tip of the line like a bottom fisherman watches a float. Also you will use this line for quite a bit of dry fly fishing which at times can be both satisfying and rewarding.

At this time, if we are lucky, the number of naturals both on the water and flying around it seems to increase day by day; to name just a few on most of the lakes I fish, the chironomids – I have counted at one time fourteen different types on a lake at the same time – all colours, all sizes – and they most likely change colour at different stages of maturity. Olives of different varieties, reed smuts, damosels, probably four different kinds of sedges, midges galore, broadwings, alders, stoneflies and hawthorn flies all start to appear from now on and I sometimes think I could go on and on naming the different ones you could possibly see, not to mention all the beetles and land born flies that get blown onto the water. I am sorry I started this list, I know it looks confusing and to be sure it doesn't help you, but it's better to know what you are up against and really it's a matter of elimination. Let's take the sedges for a start. Most anglers seeing these floppy flying fluttering insects appearing all over the water would imagine that the fish are having a beanfeast on them and waste time fishing with dry sedges the moment they start to appear. To me it's a fact that on most of the waters I fish, they are rarely taken for up to six weeks after they start becoming plentiful. Now the one thing that does take well during this period is the sedge pupa and when the fish move to take them at the surface, it's a splashy trout turning sideways sort of rise, and this pattern takes a lot of fish even when there is no apparent rise to them. After a lot of experience you will be able to recognise what the trout are taking, just by knowing the rise form. And I would remind you again that in the twenty years or so that I stomached out every trout I caught, the winged insects I found inside them were less than one per cent. I firmly believe that most insects which trout take are mainly in nymphal or larval form. Here I am referring to reservoir trout, not river fish or the trout in Irish lakes, which are a different kettle of fish altogether.

So this narrows the options down still further because most of the chironomids are very quick to pierce the surface and fly away when hatching. Not many of these are caught by the fish in the winged form. However, a lot of the chironomid larvae, although of different sizes and colours, can be imitated by a general pattern, let's say a size eight Pheasant Tail. This may sound big but I know for a fact that quite a few are over an inch long. So now we perhaps take a chance and make a selection of flies to put on our leader with a reasonable chance of at least catching a proportion of the fish available. I believe once again that not all the fish in the lake or in the area you can cover are on the same diet. Alright you may get an odd refusal, but there are plenty more fish in the sea!

Even with a selection on the leader it pays when casting to intercept an individual fish or, even if you are lucky enough to be in an area where there are plenty of fish showing, treat each fish as though it's the only one there. To my mind the worst thing you can do is to repeatedly 'line' fish, that is to frighten fish close in while attempting to cover fish further out, thus causing them to bolt outwards. You will find in a very short time that you have driven the lot out of casting range. I sometimes think that trout, like rabbits and deer, have a danger signal and rainbows especially seem to move off quickly if disturbed. Brownies seem to tolerate it up to a point, very often carrying on feeding but ignoring all offerings as if they know you are there.

I know that what usually happens is that you buy your ticket because you have heard that the place is full of fish. You go round to a spot and start tackling up and watching the water all the time until you are ready, and all you see after an hour or so is an odd fish moving too far out to cover, or sometimes no movement at the surface at all. This creates despondency, but first you must accept the fact that reservoir trout in general are not the most free of risers. A lot of the time they are bottom grubbers because in most waters the bulk of the food is down below. Of all the waters I fish, I know of only two lakes where I would say the fish are free risers. Once again, on the larger lakes there will be some spots more likely to produce a rise than others, usually in the evening.

Now we will go back a little to the situation where we are seeing no fish movement at all. This is where the long leader fishing deep and slow, with a greased fly line, and watching the end of the fly line really pays off.

I have been criticised long and often for publicising this method of catching trout and just cannot understand why. Most of the people it seems to annoy agree that, when fly fishing normally with wet fly, very many more fish take the offering in their mouths and spit it out without the angler knowing a thing about it.

My argument is this. I knew in the beginning of my trout fishing career at Eyebrook that the number of tiny tweaks I used to get while using a floating silk line cost me many a trout; purely because I was usually waiting for the accepted pull on the other end that never came to anything. I would suggest that by watching the end of the line nearest the leader, it is possible to hook every one of these fish.

Now if one retrieves the line at a moderate rate, then I would suggest that hooking the fish is relatively simple because as the fish takes the fly into his mouth, he very often turns his head to one side or other and gives an indication to the retrieving hand which is felt and reacted upon by lifting the rod. But this does not happen every time because sometimes the fish can continue towards you and will hold the fly in its mouth. This may continue until you lift to recast or the fish turns away, usually either scared by meeting shallow water or seeing some movement by the angler himself. How often do you hear a fellow angler say 'I got him on the lift', or 'It took just as my line got clear of the water'?

If you retrieve considerably faster, the take is what I call an impact take, owing to line and leader being in a straight line from the rod tip. Any deviation from this is indicated quite quickly to the hand pulling the line inwards. In both of these cases the fish hooks itself.

It's a fact of life that many, no very many, of the nymphs and larvae that fish intercept at any level in their natural environment are not, as one might think, very strong swimmers. I know, through constant observation, that most of them are at the mercy of drift, wind and wave, and are incapable of making any headway against a combination of all three. There are few actual nymphs that are true swimmers, so most of us reservoir fishermen probably fish our imitations too fast anyway, and I repeat once again that it's a good job the trout are not too clever or it would be impossible to get the returns we do. One of the typical examples is the caddis larva which crawls about the bottom inside its little tube of grit, sand and vegetation that it makes to live in. This can only crawl about the bottom, but how often we take fish when fishing with the Stick Fly, its copy, when retrieved high up in the water or even at the surface. In nature it's impossible for it to be in this place!

Are they taken for something else? I suspect that they are and most probably a lot of flies, even very good imitations, are accepted in the same way. I'm not that much of a purist to worry about it but I do believe that it is far more efficient to try to present them in the way that the fish expect to find them. This method of fishing has caught more fish for me under what are usually termed 'impossible' conditions than any other way.

Now back to basics. The tackle is the line that you have greased right to the point of the fly line – 18ft leader, Pheasant Tail size eight on point, size ten Amber Sedge Pupa on first dropper and a twelve Black Spider on top dropper.

Concentration is the essence of catching trout. Here Arthur Cove is keeping his eye on the end of the line.

Let's imagine that we are in a bay with a very slight breeze from left to right. There is a very slight ripple looking as though it's going to go flat as it usually does towards evening at this time of year. The only fish we can see are way out. Putting the mud on the leader, cast out as far as possible and allow the flies to settle and wait for them to sink, all the time watching the end of the line for the reaction. This is the hard bit, standing doing nowt. The line will start to belly towards the right. The centre piece of line between rod tip and sunken leader is the furthest to the right, depending on the strength of the drift until even with this slight ripple, a big curve is forming until it starts to move the other end, pulling it to the right. Now, as you can imagine, this drift must be causing the nymphs to rise in the water owing to the belly increasing the speed of the far end, sometimes inducing the fish to take as they rise. Seeing as it is the first try I would let this continue until the line has bellied so far to the right that the flies are now at an angle of about thirty degrees to the right. By this time, the line from the tip of the rod is running parallel to the bank. Now start a very slow retrieve. At this moment, the point fly will not be very deep, owing to the acceleration caused by the increasing belly in the line. However, all the time you must be watching the tip of the line for any sign of it stopping or, best of all, dipping slightly to the left.

OK, so you now have it all back ready to try again. Put it out as far as possible and wait until the flies have sunk deep once more, at all times watching the far end of the line. If that belly in the line starts to go round to the right as it surely will, you must lift the end of the line at the rod end and put it upwind to the left, thereby slowing the pull on the flies caused by it. This is called mending line. You can do this repeatedly during the course of a drift round. Start the slow retrieve again when the line is once again far to your right.

Sounds boring doesn't it? Sometimes it can be, because the concentration needed under these conditions is intense. So for a start, until you get used to the technique, only do it for say a half dozen casts and then do one or two with a retrieve as soon as your flies touch the water.

The ideal situation is with the wind behind or a total flat calm. Even after waiting a very long time to allow the tail fly to sink really deep, the takes are very often so slight that all you will notice at times is an inch dip in the end of the line. These are usually the better fish.

I suggest you practise this method on a water that is well stocked. The only way to describe the speed of the retrieve is that, when you have a few minutes to spare on a flat calm water, grease the leader and put a small piece of cotton wool on the point and when you can retrieve this without causing a wake anywhere along line or leader, you will be about right.

Remember that if you get a take with all the slack line when allowing the line to drift, cross-wind, the last thing you must do is lift the rod. First hook the fish by sliding the belly in the line upwind, or against the drift then take in some of the slack before lifting into it.

The other real advantage of this way of fishing is that you can lift off at any stage of the retrieve to cover an odd fish that may appear within range.

5   August and September

Most of the techniques I've described up to now will work from now till the end of the season, depending on weather conditions prevailing at the time, but there are a few situations that will try you, and in a couple of them I catch fish but cannot give a logical reason why. The main one which you will notice and probably be baffled by is the snail migration.

Now sooner or later during this period, you will notice fish bow waving through the surface in great quantities and, if it's reasonably calm, looking into the water you will see snails by the thousand, floating at the surface usually foot uppermost. They're all sizes and the fish take them readily, and the one thing I cannot understand is why the fish move so fast when taking them.

I first noticed this at Pitsford in the 1968 season and, although there was quite a strong wind off the bank I was fishing, on the Yacht Club side, the fish were racing at the surface in small shoals of about a dozen from bank to bank downwind and back. At this time Pitsford wasn't very well stocked for its size, so to see a lot of above normal size fish charging about was, to say the least, very unusual.

I threw everything at them, being able to move up and down the bank to intercept the shoals as they came within casting range, but with no joy. Upon closer inspection, I suddenly noticed the mass of snails in the water. At that time having a lot of Black and Peacock Spiders of all sizes in my box, I rapidly put three on the leader, greased up, and intercepted the next move of fish coming upwind fast. I tossed the flies in front of them and managed to catch one full of little black snails. That's it, I thought – cracked it. I proceeded once again to intercept the next lot. Well, I never touched another fish on those Spiders. After about an hour I got fed up. I must have put them in front of more than a thousand fish in that time (more likely a hundred fish dashing across to the Pitsford bank and back ten times!). And it wasn't that well stocked. I went back and got the old traditional fly box out, the one I use mainly in Ireland. I put a big Woodcock and Yellow on point, a couple of small Blacks on the droppers, flung them into the next shoal to arrive, gave two very sharp pulls and caught one on the Woodcock and Yellow. I then started to take toll of every fish that came within range. I never had a refusal.

Arthur Cove brings a large late season rainbow to the bank.

When I finished, I picked up a couple of snails and took them home and proceeded to tie some good copies of them. The next afternoon the fish were moving in the same way, and I chucked the floating snail imitations in front of them for an hour, all to no avail. I put on the Woodcock and Yellow and once again knocked out a limit dead quick. To be fair, I continued fishing after putting the snail imitations back on, without an offer. Why? Now this Woodcock and Yellow still works there sixteen years later when the snail appears.

Snails at Grafham

During the opening couple of years at Grafham, we all knew that snails and even small mussels featured as the main diet. Most of the fish rattled with the amount of snails in their gullets and they even used to fall out of their vents as you lifted them clear of the water. Some of the snails were quite large, even up to thumb nail size, but I never actually saw the snail migration happen there until about five years later. Once again the action of the fish was very similar to that at Pitsford.

A lot of anglers by then had good copies of snails but I found that most of them weren't very successful, catching perhaps an odd fish or two. Being a very clever lad, I decided to try my ultimate answer to the snail problem, and proceeded to tie on the old Woodcock and Yellow, without success. The number of fish I put it in front of was ridiculous.

Contrary to what you may think, when trying really hard to get distance when casting, I do occasionally catch the ground behind and consequently lost the old Woodcock and Yellow in the grass. Still having faith in it, I went back to my bag to get another, only to find that in my latest purge of travelling light I had left the stock box at home – tragedy. What does the thinking angler do next? Well I will tell you. I took off my hat and there, in among a multitude of worked out flies, was one very similar pattern that an angler had given me in Ireland the year before, a Cock Robin size ten. The only major difference being the small piece of red wool on the body close to the eye. 'Near enough' thinks I, tied it on point and put it in front of the next fish to come within range. I hooked it, and then repeated the process time and time again.

Now experience tells me that Woodcock and Yellow works at Pitsford but not at Grafham; the Cock Robin works at Grafham but not at Pitsford. I know, having spent hours trying to beat the odds at both venues. Why?

Snails at Rutland

About the third season after Rutland opened I had a phone call from a friend, telling me that there had been a massive rise of big fish in the bay at the end of the Hambleton peninsular, Barnhill Bay we called it. I had been doing very well thank you at the other end of the water, fishing the shallows at the Burley end, but when he described the bow waving action of the fish, I decided to meet him the following evening at about 7.00pm which I did, and sure enough my suspicions were proved correct. The whole of the bay was disturbed by the fish moving back and forth, pushing the water in front of them and moving fairly fast. As you can guess, I had seen it all before and on getting to the water's edge, I was not surprised to find the shallows full of buff to olive green coloured snails – hundreds of thousands of them floating at the top and in the bankside weeds. There were quite a lot of anglers already there (news travels fast, even on very big waters), but only one had taken a nice rainbow of about 4lb on a dry Wickham's Fancy. My friend decided to try Black and Peacock Spiders while I quietly tied on a Woodcock and Yellow with two Cock Robins on the droppers. When the next shoal came along the bank, I put these in front of them and pulled it fast across their noses. To say without result would be not true for every so often a fish or two would chase and swirl at them but not take. The only fish I had in the first hour was a brown of 4lb, foul hooked in the dorsal fin, which after about five minutes exciting play I returned to the water.

My friend had come back along the bank while I was reviving the fish and we had a short discussion on tactics. Finding that the Black and Peacock Spiders had produced no reaction at all, he had tried various other patterns, all to no avail, and went back to his pitch to try some more. I sat and had a think and, having caught a fair few fish down the lake on the Orange Nymph, I decided to put one on point and give it a go. The next shoal coming along the bank had it laid well in front of them and when they were about 10ft from it, I proceeded to pull in long fast jerks straight across their line of travel, whereupon one of them accelerated to intercept, stopping the pull with a wrist jarring take. For a few moments I thought it was once again a foul hooked fish, only to find, when it jumped end over end, that it was fairly hooked and, after a brief but exciting fight, I slid it ashore – a 4½lb brownie with the Orange Nymph stuck well in the corner of its mouth.

I remember thinking that it had most likely been a fluke and on despatching the fish, stood there waiting for the next group of fish to come within range. After a few minutes' wait they came along very close in, only a few yards from the bankside weed. I retreated up the bank about ten yards, laid the leader in their path and, sure enough, when they were close enough I started to pull and on the second one 'clonk', I was 'in' another nice fish, this time a rainbow of 3½lb, once again 'in the scissors'. My friend came along and I told him that the Orange was the medicine. We both had our limits before very long, all of them very good fish.

The next few weeks gave us some marvellous sport, and sadly it produced from most of the excellent fly tyers among us the usual selection of perfect snail imitations on which they were largely unsuccessful. The Orange Nymph killed fish after fish for us.

I find this very strange and am tempted to say 'ours is not to reason why', but there must be an answer. Is something else going on at the time these snails choose to float up to the surface? Why do they come to the top in any case? Are they dying? For a lot get washed up on the downwind shore. Have they got a parasite the same as shrimps? If some biologist has the answer, I'm sure we would all love to know.

The two things I do know are first that the snails do not accelerate fast across the surface, and secondly they can be, at these times, the bulk of the fish's diet.

It's small consolation to me really that I know that there is a way to catch fish under these circumstances, and I must draw a conclusion that although the three waters I quote all react better to different patterns, I must suppose that the same will apply to other waters also. Why?

Sedges

Now from the first day the weather starts to get a little warmer, you will notice these floppy winged flies fluttering around the water's edge in ones or twos at the start of the season, to massive swarms later on. They seem to reach their peak in our locality in late August and September, and they vary a lot in size and colour from water to water and area to area.

I must confess I don't know how many varieties there are, but I do know from my observations at most waters that there are dozens of them ranging from a near white variety in Ireland to a nearly black. They range in size from ¼ to 2½in long. If you travel from water to water, the number of patterns you will need can be very varied indeed in both colour and size, if you believe in matching the hatch meticulously. However, I do not attempt to do this and, although I do carry a very wide range, the reason for doing so is altogether different, for I believe that getting a fairly close copy is far more important on rivers than in reservoirs and I really only need three patterns on still water when fishing dry fly. This can sometimes be very profitable if a second rod is rigged up and kept handy when nymph fishing through the summer months.

This spare rod is made up with a floating line and a tapered leader of about 3lb breaking strain at the point with a size twelve Wickham's Fancy well oiled. The leader should be greased to within 3ft of the fly and the rest muddied so that it sinks right up to the fly itself. This is very important because if it floats, very often fish will move towards the fly and at the last moment sheer away, being put off by the leader sticking out like a sore thumb. If presented correctly into the ring of the rise, you will often see the fish turn to take it and a very slight tweak can make the difference between getting a positive take or the fish turning away, I imagine in disgust or frightened to death if you haven't muddied that last few feet. If the leader remains on top, it will cause more wake than the fly itself and the tweak you give to the fly at the right moment is no more than making the fly sort of pop on the surface rather than travel along it. Try it once or twice and you will see what I mean.

I remember many instances where this little trick has caught me many a good fish. One day while fishing at Rutland with little result, I saw a fish move about twenty yards to my right after having cast out with the deep nymph tackle. Dropping this rod onto the ground, I snatched up the dry fly rod and crept quietly along the bank. I extended line until I could cover the spot where the fish had moved and, landing most of the line on the bank, put it near enough into the right spot. I saw the fish turn back and, giving the fly a tweak, it was instantly swallowed by a 4½lb rainbow which rocketed out of the water on my tightening to it and soon streaked off about fifty yards out. He jumped twice again before getting his head down to give me an exciting fast running battle before I slid him ashore, not daring to give it that much 'stick', owing to the light leader and small fly. On trying to get the fly out, I found that it was so far down his throat that I couldn't see it. I cut off and tied another fly on the end and on returning back to my other rod, picked it up to find a 3lb brown firmly attached to it and landed this also. Let this be a warning. I could easily have had this rod dragged in and lost it.

As I have said before, the little dry Wickham's is one sure bet when sedges are about. However, I do like to keep a darker variety in my armoury which is tied with a much darker hackle and, if the grouse-wings are about, is as effective. In fact it is more often used as a back-up for the odd fish that appears when you are fishing for the trout you can't see. Versatility I call it, as opposed to later on in the season when you may get a rise that is truly composed of a real movement to the adult floating flies, which in most of the lakes that I fish does not happen very often. When it does, it can be very exciting indeed.

Sedges seem to be a restless type of insect, never sitting still for very long, scooting along the top, fluttering and skittering, usually mating or trying to mate on the surface. It seems to me that there are twenty males to one female for they (what I call) 'ball up' on the surface so that very often there is a fluttering mass of them in tight groups, all trying to do what comes naturally. To try to imitate this movement is nearly impossible. It's a good job the trout don't know this when they come up in a great slashing boil to take these balls of sedges for, like a few others, I have found that the old fashioned Worm Fly tied to fish dry with good quality cock hackles fills the bill and gets some really good sized fish at times. All this generally happens towards late evening, and in the failing light it can really get your pulse racing. Sometimes they will take it stationary and at other times they take it more readily on the move. Once again I've found that it doesn't want to be moved very fast at all, just causing a slight wake; it's probably the only time I'm tempted to fish on into the dark.

I found a good use for the Worm Fly fished dry in the early days at Grafham when I used to fish it amongst the weed beds in Savages Creek. I used to cast it into a hole in them and wait for a trout to come along and sort it out. A lot of these fish were up to the 6lb mark and having to hold them very hard indeed caused me great excitement. Strangely enough, I have never seen what I call a massive hatch of sedge at Rutland. Quite a lot do hatch from time to time, but I've never been in the right spot at the time and know they can be very localised in big waters.

The real bread and butter of taking fish when sedge are about though is by using the pupal stage of development. This produces far more fish over a much longer period of the season than the dry fly, much as I like catching them this way. Although these insects appear very often on the waters from May in ever increasing numbers, they seem on our Midland reservoirs to feature very little in the diet of most of the fish caught. I ignore them almost completely for quite a long period of the season except for the odd fish or two taken on the spare rod.

An Amber Sedge Pupa (size 12) claimed this 7lb 4oz fish from Ringstead Grange.

The Amber Pupa is one of the deadliest patterns I use and it takes large quantities of fish for me under a multitude of conditions. Backed up with the green variety I use it during certain periods to the exclusion of most of the other flies on the water.

Again I wonder if we really know that much about the habits of sedges when transferring from the pupal to adult stage, and my guess is that they stay in the pupal period for far longer than is generally thought. Accepting the fact that there are so many varieties of the natural insect, it may be possible that they don't all follow the same pattern of hatching. I once used to think that the same insect, when in the larval stage, stayed in its tube of grit and just dragged itself laboriously across the bottom by poking its head and legs out of it. But just a few years ago I found out that they actually are lively little devils and hop in and out of each other's cases, seeming to fight like cat and dog, as proved by a very good Irish film. It impressed me so much that I am now trying some completely new tyings to imitate them. If you get the opportunity to see this film, watch the sequence very closely – you'll see what I mean. They act like miniature grey squirrels.

The pupa patterns can be fished in a variety of ways and from about the middle of May to the end of the season, unless you get a cold week or two, they ought to be used far more often than they are. I believe that they are far more attractive to the fish at this stage than any other and I know they are taken far more readily.

Try fishing them very deep and slow if fish are not moving at the surface. Watch out for takes on the drop because this pattern, if tied rough enough, can invoke the most savage pulls you are likely to encounter. When you tie this pupa, never trim the seal fur with scissors. Leave it straggly with odd fibres sticking out all over it. Cruising fish should be tackled by casting well in front of the line of travel taken by the fish, generally upwind of them, and retrieved slowly across their path. It can also be very effective greasing the pupae themselves and allowing them to drift down towards the fish.

I am a great believer that most nymphal patterns can be fished 'dry' with confidence when fish are at the surface. My set up under these conditions is a normal 18ft leader and I usually start with an Amber size ten on point, size twelve Green Pupa on first dropper and size fourteen Amber on top dropper.

If they prefer the Green variety more than Amber, I will change to all Green Pupae in the same sizes as before. It's well worth trying a larger range of colours in this pattern if you move from area to area. Experience will tell which are the most effective.

I must add that sometimes a wet traditional Wickham's is effective as a top dropper which if tied right, floats for about a minute or so then is dragged subsurface by the leader sinking, and retrieved very slowly. Often this Wickham's is taken the moment it alights on the water.

There are of course much more complicated patterns of the pupae but this simple one is the most effective for me and as I have said before, the rougher you tie it, the better it fishes.

Pheasant Tail Nymph

I don't miss much and am known to spend a lot of time sifting through waterside debris. It's amazing what you find and it can provide not only clues to the insect life – it also makes all and sundry think that you are a bit on the wrong side of the wall. They tend to leave you alone and this can be a definite advantage. I cannot imagine why nearly everybody missed seeing the shucks of the chironomids that were washed up on the banks of Grafham Water during the second season. After all they were walking on them most of the time. After a big wind they were ankle deep, and during this period many were the complaints by householders in the near vicinity of the flies that were invading their homes.

These shucks were of many sizes and colours and I remember being impressed mainly by the size of some of them. The most prolific were the large ones, up to 1½in long. At this stage I was still avidly spooning the fish I caught and I noticed that there were quite a few empty shucks in their stomachs. I had seen this before at all the places I had fished and presumed that trout took them whether full or empty. Maybe the empty ones were taken by mistake, but I doubt if a trout takes anything by mistake alone. Could it be possible that a fly at or before the moment of emergence is taken and proceeds to emerge inside the trout before its stomach acids start to break it down? I think more than likely this is so.

After taking home trout that have been killed some seven or eight hours before and washing them under the tap, leaving them in the sink for an hour or so before cleaning them, on going back to complete the job I have found both nymphs and larvae of all descriptions swimming alive and well amongst the fish. There can be no doubt that these stomach acids must be very strong, and I really cannot understand how these relatively tender little insects can come through the ordeal alive. Survive though they do, and many's the clue I have got from them. I took a jar of these shucks home to have a closer look at them and decided to copy some of the larger ones, not really with the purpose of catching fish on them, but with the idea of using them as weights. Owing to the size, they could be tied on a size eight heavy wire hook to get the first dropper down deep to where I knew most of the fish were feeding.

The nearest thing I found to imitate the colour of the largest shucks was cock pheasant tail fibres which I tied on a longshank size eight hook, first of all without any ribbing whatsoever and with hare's ear as a thorax. I put half a dozen in my box and, compared to all the other nymphs there, they were positively enormous.

A few days later on going back to Grafham and due to a lack of rising fish, I decided to fish as deep as I could. I put one of these monstrosities on the point, a size ten longshank on the first dropper with a Black Pupa on top. I hoped to get the size ten down deep enough with it to be closer to the bottom and I'll never forget, on the second retrieve, getting a take which just slid away. On tightening, I was stuck to a rainbow of over 4lb and on landing it, I was surprised to find that it had taken the ruddy great Pheasant Tail on point. To say I was amazed would be the understatement of a lifetime. When I got it out of its jaw, it was quite a mess owing to being chewed. I got out number two and tied this on and repeated the exercise six times till I ran out of stock and managed to make up my 'eight' by sheer hard work with Black Pupae.

Ah well, as they say, back to the drawing board, and back home that night I decided to incorporate a rib into the dressing to beef it up a bit, because each of the previous half dozen had fallen to bits after being chewed up somewhat quickly in more ways than one. I tied half a dozen with a gold rib and the others with copper wire, for after having another look at my specimen in the jar, no sort of rib was prominent. I reversed the copper wire and pulled it well into the dressing where it could not easily be seen. Funnily enough even at this early stage I tied the Pheasant Tail with only six or seven turns round the shank to cover the whole distance from bend of hook to thorax, laying the fibres side by side rather than twisting them, for the shuck wasn't very thick at all. Most of the copies I have seen are tied with the fibres twisted which makes the body far too thick. I substituted rabbit underfur for the hare's ear, making a much neater thorax which should finish up like a small ball of fur, and fetching the surplus fibres over the top of this to make a nice neat head.

So back again to the water where I proceeded to do unholy slaughter with it. Only this time one nymph lasted a whole session. The beefing up had done its job and I found that if a few odd fibres did come adrift, this could be put right by just clipping them off.

At first the blokes I was fishing with would not believe that I was catching fish on them and, after putting them on sale in my shop, nobody would buy them. I suppose they thought that they weren't getting enough for their money! The peculiar thing I found right from the start of my nymph fishing career was that most trout fishermen didn't use them anyway. It was far easier to sell gaudy traditional flies and the heavier the dressing, the better they sold. I was usually left with the rejects and found I caught far more fish on the sparsely dressed ones in any case.

I remember standing at the bar in the Wheatsheaf at Perry one evening (this was and still is the local to the Grafham regulars), having a jar or two. The whole place was full of anglers and locals drowning their sorrows, when the landlord came out from the kitchen with a glass with a few nymphs in it, saying 'Look here Arthur, I've just got these out of those fish you gave me.' And sure enough, they were the twins virtually of the Pheasant Tail, matching it in size, shape and colour, both glass and a copy of the Pheasant Tail Nymph being passed round for inspection. With great difficulty I got the Pheasant Tail back – I think.

Well, as you can imagine, the bankside telegraph soon got humming and it wasn't long before everyone got to know that I was taking fish on a monstrous great nymph and sure enough, I was inundated with requests for it. A certain angler fishing alongside me in a certain bay, after seeing me extract fish upon fish with it, asked for one which I gave him. He tied it on and said to me 'It should have a white head.' I asked why and he replied 'I don't know, but it should have a white head.' On his first chuck he was smashed to atoms by a large fish taking it. He turned round and looked very sheepish as I said to him 'It's not a white head you want – it's a white flag.'

The gold ribbed variety caught a few fish but it wasn't anywhere near as good as the original so I stopped trying with that. During that first season the original would catch first at any time, both deep, shallow and on lighter hooks, floating even when the fish were fry feeding, fetched just under the surface with a fast figure of eight retrieve. It was, and still is, deadly. The same with fish rising to the Buzzer. As long as one retrieves the moment it hits the water, it keeps up at the right level or even greased up and fished as a dry fly. I know you're going to say how the hell can you get a size eight hook to float. Believe me, if you grease it up often enough, it will float. The following season I decided to improve upon it and tied it on some nice round bend hooks of normal length, not longshank. I took the dressing right round the bend and much nicer they looked too. It was at this time I started to use hooks of different weights to achieve what had been impossible for me before, to get nymphs to fish more or less at the depths I wanted them to. As you can understand, it was quite difficult to fish slow and shallow with a heavy hook and it took over ten years before Alan Bramley of Partridges produced just what we wanted. Not his fault I might add. Now I hope it doesn't take as long to get them to produce the hooks we want with ring eyes because I cannot see the point of up or down eyes.

As far as I know, Partridges are the only manufacturer of hooks in England now and all the efforts they have made to produce good hooks for us should be supported. I am very surprised at the number of flies, lures and so on that are sold tied on poor quality hooks. As usual, you must pay for hooks of real quality and people who use the rubbish will pay the consequences.

There are a couple of variations of the Pheasant Tail which I find useful. One is by using heron wing fibres for the body, producing a grey nymph which on some lakes is superior to the original. I know that some feathers are banned, but I live in a valley where herons abound and very often find a body under electricity cables and all sorts of birds get knocked down on the roads. It's a pity to let them go to waste.

The other variation I wouldn't be without is the black one using swan primaries dyed black as the body, ribbed with fine silver wire. This is useful in a big wind, fished near the top. All these should be tied in sizes from eight to twelve and are guaranteed to catch fish all over the world. I've had letters from New Zealand, Chile, USA, Canada and I have personally proved its worth in the British Isles and especially in Ireland.

Gold Ribbed Hare's Ear Nymph

This is a well established pattern which I have used over the years to very good effect, especially under very difficult conditions, bright sunlight, flat calms and so on.

I suppose apart from its fish catching values, I am attracted to it because it's one of those nymphs that can be tied very rough. This is always an asset in fly tying. Most of my friends when given the choice of my fly boxes seem to pick the chewed up specimens, I suppose on the assumption that I've had plenty of fish on them. I have had the experience of mates having picked what I thought to have been the neatest flies in my collection, tie them on and then tread them into the mud underfoot and when asked why, have had them reply that they look more like the ones I'd got on. The truth is that I rarely throw away any old flies unless the hook is broken. After having spent years building a collection of really good 'irons', I much prefer to keep them to strip down and retie on them. It used to be a great source of joy to me, when visiting the office of *Trout Fisherman*, to be shown 'new' patterns sent in by budding inventors, which I had discarded after trying many years ago, and on going home, could produce them from one of my old stock boxes from way back.

From all I've read, the Hare's Ear is a fly to imitate the olives, a fairly common fly in most of the British Isles. The pattern is from way back in fly fishing history, and was mainly used in the old days as a dry fly. As a nymph, it is in my opinion an asset to any reservoir fisherman's armoury, and should be tried in all sizes from longshank tens to normal size fourteens, a very wide range indeed. Many times it has proved its worth for me.

I remember once going to Church Hill Farm one late afternoon and being told that most of the anglers had been there all day and that very few had taken fish. I pulled out three good fish in half an hour. Bright sunshine, flat calms and the Gold Ribbed Hare's Ear go together. Tie it with a gold rib prominent and the fur picked out from between with a needle.

Orange Seal's Fur Nymph

I devised this pattern many years ago after watching some small insects hatching at Eyebrook, which after emerging from the shuck, actually changed colour from a grey to orange in a very short time while pumping their wings up. I surmised that at this stage they were most vulnerable, which proved to be right for I had many fish on them, in those days tied on size twelve and fourteen.

I have a very strong suspicion that a lot of our insects change colour at some stage of emergence and know for a fact that this applies to the great lake olive (this is the large one that usually appears on the Midland waters in early spring and late autumn). I've never seen them when the water starts to get warm, when the olives are generally the smaller varieties.

This is one of the only nymphs I tie with seal's fur to which I give a haircut. When I finish tying it I trim the body fur into a nymph shape, tapering from bend to thorax, and once again make the gold rib prominent.

I tie it in many sizes from ten longshank down to fourteen normal shank. I have fished it in a varying range of depths from slow and deep to greased up to fish like a dry fly. Try it with a size ten longshank greased up floating on top in a flat calm, just giving it the occasional tweak. Fish seem to appear from nowhere to attack it. Both rainbows and browns love it and, as a top dropper in a size twelve for late evening browns, we have done murder with it.

I remember giving one to an acquaintance to try, and on meeting him again a week or so later, he told me that he had used it at Latimer Park fishery and as soon as it hit the water, fish grabbed it every time – and not another soul was catching fish.

Some Dos, Don'ts, Risks and Perils of Playing Fish

If you really lay on the pressure with side strain, you'll stop even the biggest fish from running far.

Be doubly sure to keep a tight line when playing a fish at long range.

Brinkmanship.

The perils of using an ultra-long leader. Arthur Cove says he should have backed up the bank and beached this fish. However, things were going well so he took a chance and grabbed hold of the leader. That time it worked.

Releasing a fish. Keep it in the water, grab the hook and let the trout do the rest . . . It usually works.

6 Conditions

Drift

To call any type of lake fishing, still water fishing, is the biggest mistake anyone can make, for no expanse of water is ever still and until the angler begins to understand this vast movement of water, I don't think he will be very successful in locating and catching fish. The simplest way I can describe this movement is by asking you to use your imagination.

Standing on the upwind shore of a large lake with the wind at your back, let's say for the sake of simplicity that there is a very strong wind, a ripple and sometimes a piece of flat water close to the bank. This small ripple increases to a wave further out, getting to larger waves even further away and developing into big rollers crashing into the down-wind shore. In places like Grafham and Rutland I have seen waves of four feet or more on a particularly rough day. Now this vast mass of water, millions of tons of it in rapid motion at the surface going downwind, must return to its starting point, otherwise we would be able to advance with it or behind it without getting our feet wet.

This causes an undercurrent coming back at a lower level which replaces the water on the upwind shore. Its force is apparent if you look at the erosion caused on even quite small waters by the undermining of banks and bank collapse, which eventually forms quite steep cliffs in only a short time, especially at Graffham.

Now imagine we are standing on a point half way down the same water with the wind from left to right and this rolling wave. Obviously the water is usually shallower just in front of us and to each side of us, because on a normal lake it's rare to get a steep drop off from a point, for they usually extend from dry land gradually to deeper water further out. Let's ask ourselves a question. If this mass of water bears down on this point, moving at great speed and suddenly meets the shallows, why doesn't it build up and cause a wall of water off this point? The answer to this really is gravity, in the fact that the only way the water can keep its level is by speeding up over the shallows, much in the same way as you would squeeze the end of a hose pipe to cause a jet of water to come out of the end with greater force. Hence over the shallow point,

This demonstrates fishing along the bank. Note the effect of wind on line (*see* Fig 11).

the water is moving much faster. This is why you need a much longer leader to get anywhere near to the bottom if any amount of drift is present. On this particular pitch I have in mind, knowing that it is only about four feet deep thirty yards out, I have fished with an 18ft leader with quite a heavy nymph on point and haven't touched bottom at any time while the drift persisted.

Now this can cause, especially round the downwind side of a point, a current as the water spreads out on meeting deep water again, a type of whirlpool with water coming back on itself, especially if there is a bay on the downwind side of the point. This back eddy can trap a lot of insects that would normally be pushed down drift to the shore. I can give a couple of marked instances of this, knowing full well that in a wind of a certain direction on Rutland water there is such an eddy round the point of the Hambleton peninsular that a boat drifting, although under the sheltered bank, will go in circles (and those boats are quite big with a heavy inboard engine). Another place where there is a marked effect is the little peninsular they built to preserve Normanton Church. These places at the right time can hold a vast amount of fish.

It seems to take a long time for most people to understand this movement, but once you begin to understand it you should be able to make it work to your advantage. Fish use this drift as fish in a stream and in the early days at Grafham a few knowledgeable people experimented with echo sounders and fish finders. They came to the conclusion that the fish moving slowly upwind at the surface, usually feeding, upon meeting the shallow water on the upwind bank, moved back down the lake at a much deeper level, moving very fast.

I can't impress upon you too much the force of these currents and

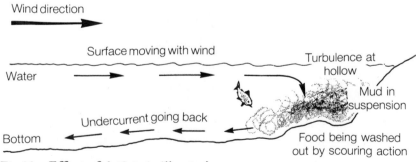

Fig 11 **Effect of drift in 'stillwater'**
Despite the name, stillwaters are never still. Here can be seen one of the effects of current on the bankside.

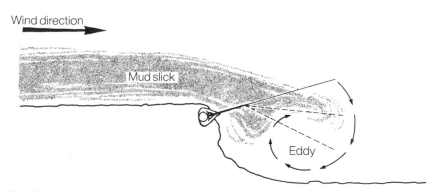

Fig 12   **Fishing a mud slick**
The food is being sucked into the eddy created by the
wind. The turbulence of the eddy causes the insects on the
bottom to be washed out and up. This nearly always
happens on a point, which is why points often produce
more fish.

well remember at times when boat fishing, drifting on a collision course
with one of the towers usually present in most drinking water reservoirs, and not even bothering to pick up the oars, knowing full well that
the current would push us one side or the other of it.

Even when the big wind abates, this drift keeps the water moving for
quite a long time and, although the surface looks flat calm, it still moves
at an appreciable rate.

The situation I have just described can mean very good fishing if you
have the knowledge to take advantage of it. In the first place, fish tend
to be much more active after a big blow owing probably to a greater
oxygen content in the water or a mass of insects and nymphs being
stirred out of their places of abode, or even land based insects being
blown onto the water. Whichever it is, it certainly makes the job much
easier for, if fish are on the move, they are usually looking for trouble
and if they meet me they find it.

Now let's keep the imagination going and while the big wind is still
keeping the waters on the move, I will often position myself just round
the corner of the point where it is clear or along the edge of the
coloured water that is caused by the silt stirred up by the fast current
coming over the shallows. I place my team of nymphs down and slightly
across wind to come round with the drift swinging across the divide
between the rough water and the calm sheltered water, trying to get this
natural swing as slow as possible just over the clear water. Fish seem to
hang along this line, I suppose taking the food that is being sucked into
the eddy behind the point. If it is warm you will often see fish move

along this line and it is sometimes more profitable to fetch the nymphs closer to the surface by dabbing four or five blobs of grease on the leader, one about a foot above the point fly and one each side of the droppers at about the same distance. Remember that, owing to casting much more downwind than across, you will be on a fairly tight line when a fish takes so don't do anything violent when you see a boil anywhere near your leader. Just lift slowly until you make contact. The most profitable way to use this technique is not to cast too far across wind so that the flies are caused to accelerate wildly across the drift. A movement of about six feet by the point end of the line is ample and then just stand and let the fish do the rest. Easy isn't it? If you don't see any fish movement, just retrieve very slowly up the edge of the clear water.

The next stage is when the water has calmed down more into a ripple and the silt starts to settle down. In some lakes it disappears more rapidly than others, and you can then cast a bit more square across wind, allowing the nymphs to have a far greater movement than before. A lot depends on the strength of the drift, for I don't believe that allowing the flies to whip round quickly at the end of the drift catches many fish at all. In fact I find it tends to put them off taking until they are once again in a straight line with the line itself. Of course, if you see fish at the surface, use the grease again, remembering that after a time the grease manages to transfer itself along the whole length of the leader and when this happens, degrease the whole leader and start again. Experience taught me a long time ago that fish don't like this showing like a cable across the surface. The real object of applying the grease in small blobs is to enable the leader to keep the nymphs up on or near the surface for a limited period until dragged down by the ungreased parts of the leader. This allows a slow retrieve without causing a wake on the surface. *This is very important* and it's the difference between success and failure. For the same reasons it is sometimes more expedient if the composition of the nymphs allows you to keep them at the top by greasing them (the nymphs) only, but not putting grease on the leader at all. By this I mean that if the nymph has enough body to carry plenty of grease, such as a pattern tied with seal fur, it will absorb a fair amount. After it's dragged down by the sunken leader it can be retrieved without causing wake, which in turn is controlled by the speed or lack of it to prevent it.

The next stage in the sequence is the water having calmed down to an apparently motionless flat. On casting square across what was the wind sometime before, you may (or may not) be surprised to find that although it looked calm, it still has quite a strong drift. Unless another wind occurs, this can continue in the prevailing direction for quite a few days, weakening all the time.

To me this is the best time of all, for by casting a team of nymphs across this drift with the leader sinking, I can cover a vast amount of water, letting the drift do the job for me and with good control by mending the line nearest the rod tip, can to some extent allow them to move at what speed I like. The method is to try to keep it at the same speed as the current and the takes are indicated either by the line stopping or deviating from the true drift or, best of all, by the line being dragged against the drift. These are usually the better fish. Once again, nothing violent, just tighten to them slowly. *Strike* is not in my trout fishing vocabulary.

The joy of this method of fishing is fairly apparent. One doesn't have to do very much at all physically. Lay your line across the drift, keep it under control, watch the end of the line like a hawk, have a quiet smoke and let the fish do the rest. The only violent thing you will do is knock fish on the head, and if you don't want to do that then unhook them without taking them from the water and let them go. If you are fishing without much success under these conditions, experiment with the length of leader. If you are touching bottom occasionally, I wouldn't bother too much, I would suspect every time it did this that I was into a fish and react accordingly. Strange how many times the bottom has moved. However, if you don't touch it occasionally, add another six feet to your leader. This is quite easy to do without too much bother by cutting off the first dropper completely, then the point fly. Then take the spool of nylon you should have in your waistcoat pocket, cut about seven feet off, put the spool back in your pocket and water knot this length to the end of your original leader which is still attached to the line, using one end of it as the new first dropper. Simple isn't it? The knot left by the original first dropper is no trouble at all. The only snag is that while doing this, you usually put your nymphs on the ground and can't find them. Do as I tell you – when you cut them off, stick them in your hat.

The other method to get the point fly to go deeper is to put on one tied on a heavier hook. If you have already done this and still can't get down, add another six feet by the original method. I occasionally use leaders up to 30ft long with no trouble at all. Once again, if fish are showing, you won't have this problem. Just lay your flies about 15ft updrift of them and retrieve slowly. Do not use the grease on the leader in a flat. If you have to use it, grease the nymphs only, or change over to the lightest nymphs you've got. The smaller they are, usually the higher in the water they stay.

GALES

Now sometimes it just isn't possible during a gale to get into the spots you would like, owing usually in my case to getting to the water late. If the wind is still strong, although I don't like facing into it, I will, if forced to, and for an hour or so will put up with it, usually with varying degrees of success. The best situation to pick under these conditions is where one can find a steep drop straight off the bank. Owing to the turbulence it's essential that you can put your flies into clear water and as you can understand, if it is shallow, there is usually too much muddy water to get over.

If you have picked the right spot, there's no need to attempt to cast a long way out, for under atrocious conditions ten yards is ample. As I have told you before, I use six and five double taper lines and I can get out plenty far enough to catch fish, for invariably they are at your feet.

My own best performance under these conditions was at Whitwell Creek one foul night with rain and a raging gale. There was no room on the sheltered side of the creek, so I was forced, luckily as it turned out, to fish right into the teeth of the very strong gale. I rigged up with a Pheasant Tail on point and two Black Spiders, fishing as deep as I could under these conditions. After an hour, I took a beautifully conditioned brownie of 3½lb on the big nymph. The fish were there alright, but it took me another ten minutes to work it out, for all of a sudden I saw a big boil in the side of a wave, lifted the rod and was stuck into a big rainbow which had taken one of the Black Spiders on the drop. Well, a nod's as good as a wink; I slid it ashore, 4lb. After replacing the Pheasant Tail nymph on point with another Black Spider, I greased up the leader and punched it back out into the waves which were by this time about three footers. It went all of ten yards, which was as far as I could cast. I remember seeing the cast enveloped by a big wave, lifted slowly and was into another slab of silver which shot out about forty yards, rolled over and went deep. After a few minutes I got it under control and fetched it to hand – 4½lb rainbow. The next five casts produced five more fish, all of a good size, giving me a limit of over 30lb. Yes the fish were there all right, mopping up drowned and hatching chironomids by the thousand, even being washed ashore at my feet. I guess most of my casts were not further than eight yards. A short one into an area where fish are is better than a long one into blank water.

There is another situation where you can profit if you manage to get the bank space when a big wind is blowing, and that is by casting across the wave, usually with a greased up leader. If you've got the room, walk downwind with it, keeping pace with the line. Sometimes you can go quite a long way, at other times the fish won't let you, for when the line sails outwards, you're in business.

The black bodied Pheasant Tail is a good one to use on the point under these conditions of a big rolling wave. Under an even ripple, the three Black Spiders seem to do the trick and of course if the sedges are about, especially if it is warm, the Amber Sedge Pupa will work. A few minutes spent in observation can give you the clues to real success. This is why I never put a fly on the leader until I've had a good look. The real lesson is to make use of the drift to your advantage. It's no use trying to fight it.

Scum Lanes

There is another freak of nature that most anglers don't take full advantage of, and these are what we call scum lanes. These are the lines of flat water which usually appear once the water starts to warm up. They are like highways to feeding trout, always running up and downwind between the waves on ripples. They act like flypaper because most of the insects stick to these lanes like glue.

In a big wind there can be dozens of them, usually pretty close together, and in a ripple they are wider apart and are bigger. Sometimes the fish favour a particular one, especially when there are a lot of them, and I have found the average is about one in six. This doesn't create any problem though, for usually you can see the fish moving up them and, if they are close together, you can cast across quite a few of them. The most killing way to get fish to take on them is to cast across into the rough water and retrieve your flies through this into the lane.

When they are wider, and I must admit I like them this way the best, you must find a place where they are close enough to the bank to be able to cover the whole lot, as sometimes the fish move only on the outer edge of them. I don't think the fish do this knowingly, it's just that the insects are thicker on the ground there.

What causes them is not known to me and as far as I can make out, nor to anyone else. Once, when on a panel of so-called experts, one of our number answered that they were caused by projections on the shore. I nearly fell off my chair, for if this was the case, then with the wind in the same direction they would always appear, which they don't.

They sometimes happen on the sea and I've seen them in the English Channel when over the Varne Bank while cod fishing. Another theory is that they are formed by currents thrown up from the bottom. I can't agree with this either for the same reason as before, for with the drift in one direction they would be there more frequently and we would be able to forecast their appearance, which we cannot.

There are ways to make artificial scum lanes. One simple way is to tip a cup of tea or coffee into the water when there is a ripple on the water. If this is done slowly enough, the oil in the milk will cause the water to flatten, killing the wave or ripple, and on being blown downwind, a lane of calm water will appear. Of course if you just throw it in, it causes a large flat area that just goes away from you with the wind. There are other ways of doing this which I will not mention here, but the method above does not produce fish on them like the natural.

My own theory is that they are caused by daphnia or algae multiplying rapidly. They are full of protein and produce enough fat or oily substance to kill the ripple or wave. They are more general in their appearance when the water has warmed up and are held in division by the surface drift. They are always running downwind, never across. Anyway, whatever causes scum lanes, make good use of them whenever possible. One early morning, driving along the far bank at Eyebrook with a friend, I saw a scum lane running along the bank with a vast quantity of fish moving on the outside edge. This was a solitary lane about ten yards wide stretching from the corner of the dam right along the Rutland bank and going right down to the Leicestershire end. I didn't say a word and waited until my friend noticed it. Suddenly he wrenched the steering wheel to the right, drove up the steep bank and stopped between two trees with the van parked at a crazy angle, jumped out and said 'come on' and started to throw tackle out sharpish like.

I didn't see what all the rush was about. There were only a few anglers about and they were mainly on the dam and the other bank. So tackling up quickly we were soon at them, my friend getting in immediately opposite where he had 'parked' and I going about forty yards back up towards the dam. We had a couple of hours' good fishing and my friend shouted to me 'tea' and I went back to the van where he had opened the back and laid his fish out in a row on the floor. What a lovely sight they made. Eleven brownies, from 1lb to 1lb 14oz. So while he lit the stove and put the kettle on, I laid mine alongside them – nineteen fish, all brownies, no rainbows there in those days. Mine were from 1½lb to 2lb 12oz. He remarked when putting the brew gear away that I always get the better fish. I told him that I probably had a shoal of bigger fish in front of me anyway. And we decided to swap pitches as the scum lane was still there.

Now I had taught this chap to fish right from the start and he was using the same tackle and nymphs as myself. He cast exactly the same as myself, there was no possible reason why I should average out with a better class of fish and, after another couple of hours, we came back again to compare our catch and I still had the bigger fish – luck.

Another tale concerns this same bloke, and the same water, although on the other side of the lake. Many visitors to Eyebrook will know the spot – my friend was fishing in the mouth of the ditch that runs in along the roadside, and I was fishing about thirty yards to his left towards the point, or tongue as it was called in those days. We had a few fish apiece when I noticed he was obviously casting to a fish that was about twelve yards in front of him. You tend to notice things like this because he, like myself in those days, was a maximum distance caster and it wasn't very often we didn't put out thirty yards or more.

This carried on for about half an hour, me keeping a weather eye on him occasionally between fishing out my own casts, which I wasn't doing with much conviction, owing to him distracting my attention by still persisting in casting short. So I decided to go up and see what he was up to. On getting close to him, he backed up a few yards putting his finger to his lips and whispered 'Take a look at this.' On approaching stealthily, I saw what it was all about, for there lying alongside the weeds that come out from the ditch hovered a brown trout with its tail towards us, obviously quite huge. He told me what I already knew – that he had been casting at it for ages. He invited me to 'have a go' which I did, putting my nymph, a Green and Yellow, between the weed and slightly beyond it, not showing the line to it at all, just the three flies landing in its line of vision. It surged forward, taking what I thought was the point fly and on me tightening to it, shot into the air and tumbled end over end outwards, jumping again about twenty-five yards out. It was then I noticed the point fly dangling as it cleared the surface by about four feet. I just said 'Hell', for I then knew it was on a size fourteen dropper, a Black Pupa which in those days, as we tied them with the dressing right round the bend, didn't give much chance of the point going home very far. I took it very easy from then on and after another couple of heart-stopping moments as it jumped end over end (I wonder why browns only jump like this – rainbows seem to jump out clean and dive head first back in or even more exciting, stand on their tails, a thing I've never had a brown trout do), I finally beached it, to find the little Black Pupa firmly gripped in the scissors. I knocked it on the head and my friend, looking at it lying on the grass said 'What a beauty, near six pounds.' It was one of those trout with spots as big as your thumb nail, and turning it over he said 'Bloody Nelson, it's only got one eye, how did you know that?'

I could never convince him that I didn't know that it was blind in the left eye. This was the side he was casting, being scared of getting his team caught up in the weeds, and hadn't ventured a cast on the other side. Luck? When I see him occasionally, he usually winks at me, always with his left eye.

Weeds

Most anglers seem to complain for some reason or other and in some instances quite rightly so, but I can never see the reason for complaining about weed growth in reservoirs. I sometimes think that anglers do not take the very obvious advantage of it, for it not only provides shelter and breeding places for the insects that live in them, it also provides cover for the fisherman. Soon after Pitsford opened, the weeds started to become prolific and among the many moans was the one that you couldn't fish a fly through clean, or that it was a job to reach open water. But if you use your loaf, it can be much more help than hindrance. I know it has enabled me to get quite a lot of fish that I would otherwise never have been able to get anywhere near. All it requires is what I call my old friend versatility, for during the times at Pitsford when the moaning was at its worst, I was doing very well. One of the reasons why this was so was because it kept a lot of anglers away from these banks, leaving them so quiet that it was possible to have up to four or five hundred yards of bank to myself.

Now these weed beds had holes in them, some larger than others, but if there was room to put a team into them, these holes always had a resident or two. I can hear your brains ticking over, wondering how it is possible to put a team of nymphs into a hole in the weeds not more than a yard round and retrieve far enough to attract a fish without getting caught up in them. The simple answer is, you don't retrieve at all. Aha, then how do I get enough movement to catch 'em then?

This ploy works for me and, if you use it, once again the softly softly approach works wonders.

Imagine once again that in a mass of weed there is a gap or hole with weed in it a foot or two beneath the surface. Sometimes you may see a fish move, sometimes not. However, you will not find out unless you try, and believe me, they are there more often than not. Now the object

April Fool's Day, 1976. Lots of fish were to be had amongst this
rubbish and weed at Pitsford. In these conditions a short line is
essential.

I try to achieve is to use a heavy nymph on point and, using a reasonably
short leader, I have the first dropper only about a yard above it. I drop
the point fly onto the outer edge of the growth above the surface and
use this as an anchor so that the dropper is in the open water in the hole.
Now if you've degreased the leader as I always do, you may get a
reaction from the fish almost immediately. If not, just retrieve gently
until the line tightens, pulling the leader just enough so that the anchor
(in this case it's the heavy nymph), is now held by the weed and gently
strum the line, now reasonably taut, making the dropper rise and fall
gently in the hole. You can keep this up until you either attract a fish or
get fed up and go and try another hole, but I think you will be surprised
at the number of fish you will entice.

The next problem, once having hooked a fish in one of these

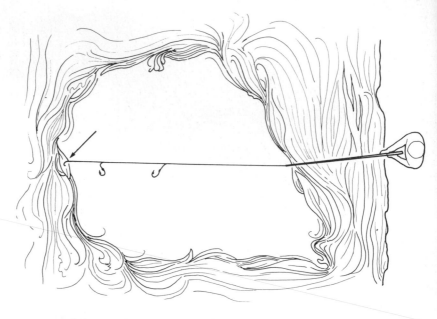

Fig 13   **Fishing a hole in the weeds**
The point nymph is anchored in weed furthest away. The
line is tightened to the rod tip and then gently strummed to
attract fish to the droppers.

situations, is getting it out, and even this is far easier than you will
imagine. It's no time for playing to the gallery. In a situation like this
you must be very firm and keep the fish's head pointing upwards and
pull, yes *pull* it towards you, and if the water is shallow enough on your
edge of the hole, let him get his head into it. They usually dive into it
and most assuredly get a clump of weed wrapped round the leader
close to the head. Keeping the leader up, let this slide over its eyes.
When in this state it usually lies still for now it cannot see where to go.
Advance and pick it out.

If the water is too deep to get near the fish, then you must be quite
strong willed (I was going to put 'brutal') but with a very firm hand,
keep the fish right at the top and slide it over the weeds so that you get it
close enough to grab it. All well and good you say, but what if it jumps?
If it does, as far as I am concerned it helps me to get it in quicker, for
while it's out of the water it's easier to pull. You try it. I've had hundreds
of fish this way.

Another approach under these conditions is to use a dry fly. I would
suggest a Wickham's Fancy once again. I know that at one time I used

Make use of the natural weed cover and always keep below the sky line when fishing a short line.

to walk up from the diversion dam at the Holcot end towards the gorse bushes with just eight dry Wickham's stuck in my pad on my waistcoat and walk back an hour or so later with eight fish.

Peter O'Reilly, the Irish Trout Fishery officer, will remember me pulling out a rainbow from a narrow run in the weed in Whitwell Creek, using the anchored nymph method and that run was only a foot wide – 4½lb that one was. Many of the fish taken from Savages at Grafham were allowed to bury their heads into the weed to blindfold them.

Also, consider the algal scum that can get washed in and collect in thick masses in very hot weather. It is used by fish as shade and it is well worth your while using the same method, for very often they will shoot out from under it to swallow your offerings, and in quite shallow water too.

Later on in the season the fish start taking the very small fry, just when they hatch – pinheads I call them. The fish herd them up against the edges of the weed beds appearing in great swirls very close in to them. Try a greased up Pheasant Tail Nymph tied on a number ten longshank hook. If you apply Permagrease often enough it will eventually float. They pick it off like a dry fly, for I believe many of the forays that trout make are just to stun them. Thus injured the fry are easy meat for the trout when it swims back to get them. Another good dodge when it's really bright and when they are on the pinheads is to use a Kingfisher Butcher, again greased up. If this is left floating in the vicinity of this frenzied action it will be taken quite violently. This is a wet fly with a gold body and it actually floats on its side. I never could fathom out why they take it so well, but take it they do. Another time when fish seem to take the dry fly well is late on in the season when the weeds have died down and most of them have sunk to the bottom, leaving brown patches floating, although anchored, and the fish are after the larger fry. Very often they will take the Wickham's. Sit within a yard or two of the shelters once again. For the water gets cleaner as it gets colder. You can see the fish coming and give that fatal tweak I have mentioned before. Once again I have had many good fish this way, even after the first frost.

Dry Fly Fishing

The dry fly is a strong arrow in my armoury and I think it is wrong to imagine that all the dry flies I use are what are generally accepted in the true sense as conventional. In principle, it's a method of catching trout when there is a hatch of natural fly on the water and fish can be seen rising to them. Not so really, for very often fish can be attracted up to them when no insect can be seen at the surface. One imagines a beautiful little fly with a lovely pair of wings sticking upright with shiny stiff little cock hackles – a sight to behold. Much as I like my collection of dry flies, I have known for a long time, over thirty years now, that most of my rough offerings of nymphs have in the main produced far more fish than all the dry flies put together, and by this I mean actually greasing them to float on or in the surface film. Fished this way, I get far fewer refusals with them than with the real medicine, for fished wrongly the dry fly, whatever pattern, can be a great attractor but a bad taker, and if you don't believe me go to your nearest water and put one on. If you are inexperienced with them you will find a great number of fish coming to them, sometimes with a good swirl, and when you lift there's nothing stuck on the other end. I also know that sometimes when this happens, if you leave the fly which now usually is below the surface, the fish will take again, often either hooking or getting a contact. Now I think I can help you to some extent when using a 'pukka' dry fly, then will go on to explain how to use nymphs dry, sometimes more successfully than in the conventional way.

The tackle I use is composed thus – the normal rod, with the fly line greased right to the top including the butt piece, for the reason that all plastic floating fly lines are basically sink tips, in my case owing to the tapered portion sinking after one or two immersions. The leader, which in this case isn't too long (8ft is plenty long enough, the main part of which is a continuous taper down to about 5lb breaking strain), with a tippet which is another piece of level nylon usually about 2½lb break-ing strain. This is knotted to the end of the main leader and from now on is called the tippet. The water knot is the one to use, and clip both ends off short. My leader usually finishes up about 10ft long.

If you buy your flies, most are tied with upturned eyes, this being traditional. Much as I admire it, I thought long ago that it's about time we did away with it as far as hooks are concerned. For I am convinced that if all hooks were made with a ring eye, it would not only make them a fraction cheaper, but would not detract from their hooking qualities. It would also be much easier to tie them on, for with such small flies with a stiff hackle, usually as far as possible forward towards the eye, most people I know have a problem tying them to the leader. I have used this method for this type of fly for years and it's never let me down yet – push the end of the tippet through the eye, slide the fly up the nylon, then tie a knot in the end and trim the excess dead short. Then make a running noose with a simple overhand knot, keep the noose long enough to be able to put on the fly which is fetched down again, towards the end through this noose you've just made. Moisten the nylon between finger and thumb, then slowly tighten the noose steering it between the upturned eye and hackles by pulling the tippet at right angles to the shank of the hook, using it to steer the loop behind the eye of the hook. Once the loop is smaller than the diameter of the hackles, pull down till it is tight. This way I find it's not possible to trap the hackles, causing them to spread at all angles. It's well worth practising this knot. I know a lot of people use the tucked half blood knot, but this one usually makes the fly sit much neater on the water, purely because it cannot neck (this is when the nylon slides round at right angles to the fly). So far, so good. You're nearly ready to start.

All dry flies should be treated with Permaflote before being put in your boxes. I would suggest you do it again once the fly is on the end of the leader by opening the bottle and lowering the fly into the liquid (I wish Fred Buller would use clear glass in the bottle) and allowing to dry. Do not use until it is fully dry. Replace the cap tightly on the bottle as this preparation evaporates quite quickly if left exposed to air.

Now get a piece of clay, mud or sinking agent, between finger and thumb and muddy the whole of the tippet thoroughly. Do a trial cast onto the water close in so you can see that the fly is sitting on the water correctly and the tippet sinks. If it doesn't, in the first case retie your knot; in the second use some more mud on the tippet. If it does you can start one of the most delightful forms of trout fishing I know of.

If you are in luck and can see trout rising, move along quietly towards them using all the cover you can find. I try to keep behind bushes or bankside weeds or big tussocks of grass until I get within ten yards or so of the fish. This is the time to forget all about long distance work and deliver the fly gently into the ring of the closest fish. Now the water may be flat, as it usually is when trout start to move on most waters. Use the disturbance they make when rising to cover the delivery of your fly to them. Don't land your fly line into the ring, just the fly and leader. I promise under these conditions you won't wait long for a reaction and, depending on how they are taking, sometimes you must lift fairly sharply. At other times you must wait until the thick part of the leader starts to slide away. Two or three casts at them in trial and error will show you how. I personally am prepared to miss the first two. You will soon get the hang of it, not forgetting that you are on a much finer piece of nylon than you've used before and that these reservoir fish can run big. My largest on dry fly was a 7lb 12oz rainbow at Ringstead Grange on a size fourteen. I have found from experience the bigger they are, the more likely they are to swallow it. Short of being broken, most of the small flies are well down the throat and I suggest that when you do land a fish, tie a fresh fly on and leave the used one to dry in your hat.

The tippet can be renewed when it gets too short by knotting another length on after cutting close to the original knot. When you cut off the fly, leave at least an inch of nylon outside the eye of the hook so that you can push it back through the eye, and it usually springs off the eye quite easily. If it doesn't, use a needle to open out the noose, otherwise you will have a lot of dry flies with their eyes blocked with pieces of nylon that you cannot move.

Again in a flat calm, if there is no real rise to anything at the surface, it takes much more concentration to beat the odds and I know of a few dry fly fanatics who just cast out and sit and wait until a fish commits suicide. That's not my idea of fishing, it's a bit like legering on top. I watch the flies like a hawk, and any movement in the vicinity is responded to by tweaking which usually brings the desired result. The muddied part of the tippet does not sink that deep and, if you pull gently on the line, the fly just seems to pop up on its hackles and not move along at all. Choice of fly is important, and under most conditions a small grey dry Buzzer is very good and once again, if the sedge is on the water, the Wickham's is the best bet. However, you will probably find the fly that suits your own water best but these two flies, size twelve and fourteen, work the best in a big ripple, or in a wave size ten.

There are a few occasions when you can use much bigger patterns – just to mention two that have been successful for me, the Damosel and the Daddy Longlegs. I used to think especially on the larger waters, that the bright blue damosels that flew and hovered above the water never featured much in a trout's diet. I have however found over the last couple of seasons on the smaller waters that when they are plentiful, usually when there is nothing else about in any quantity, trout will take these gaudy flies quite avidly.

I usually watch for the signs of them being taken in a splashy rise, sometimes the fish jumping right out of the water to intercept them. I then cast in the near area, retrieving in a smooth action making a fair wake on top. It usually fishes best in the vicinity of rushes.

The Daddy, my favourite of the larger flies, is deadly at times and is probably one of the most neglected land born flies of the lot on this side of the Irish Sea. Anyone going over to Ireland had better learn to use them or they will at times miss the best sport of the season. If most anglers over here used it more often, especially on the big reservoirs, they would be surprised at the number of fish that come for them. There are many ways of fishing the many patterns. Sometimes the fish like them stationary, sometimes moved quite fast, and they are easily fished from the bank. I must confess, the easiest way is in a big wind behind, casting out as far as possible and feeding line out to let it drift away downwind, or position yourself on a projecting bank and let it swing round in a good ripple. Many a great boil has resulted in a positive take if left alone under these conditions.

I went to Ringstead Grange about 7.00pm one Sunday evening a few years ago and asked one of the very many anglers how it was fishing. I was told that although plenty of fish had been moving all day, only two fish had been caught. I just couldn't understand this as moving fish are feeding fish and, upon standing there for a few minutes, I noticed a daddy blown over my head. It crash landed on the ripple about ten yards out and was instantly gobbled up. I went back to the car, made up my rod, tapered leader as I've described, put on a well oiled Daddy, walked back to the water's edge and asked the same bloke I'd spoken to before if I could have a chuck. It was quite crowded for many good fish come out of this water, and he said yes but I wouldn't do any good because he'd fished there all day.

While he was talking, another one was taken right in front of him and mine soon landed close by in the ripple to be instantly taken by a 2½lb rainbow which cavorted all over the place. After landing this I moved a few yards to the left and had another instantly. To cut an exciting hour short, it was not long before I had six fish, all over 2lb, and gave the fly to a young lad fishing along the bank. I hope he caught on it. I went off rather quickly, one of the few times I've felt embarrassed, for how can anyone, especially fishing with their backs to the wind, miss seeing such large flies being blown onto the water and being taken, and not understand what is happening. It not only embarrasses me, it amazes me as well. As I've said before, most of the clues are fairly obvious.

On most waters there is no objection to using the natural and three or four of these on a size eight hook look very attractive and, although quite a mouthful, are taken well. I loved drifting along an Irish lough with Lal Faherty of Lough Corrib. He certainly showed me how effective the natural can be with a blowline or dapping line and I know the fish one can take at times with it used as a top dropper on a team of flies as demonstrated by Peter O'Reilly. He gets a lot of fish on it and sometimes uses two on the same leader.

Now one of the most popular nymphs I use as a dry fly is the Pheasant Tail Nymph, and I know that the commercially tied patterns are difficult to make float because they tend to use heavy hooks. They are usually tied on longshank hooks, and this is all the more reason for anglers to tie their own because in tying most flies there are little tricks you learn when you want to make what I call dual purpose flies – that is a nymph that can be used normally or greased to fish as a dry fly. This can be quite easily done by putting a pinch of fur behind and under the hackle so that when treated with either Muscilin or Permaflote there is this receptacle there to absorb it, so making a very durable fly. I've done this for years and you can imagine the number of people who have inspected my fly boxes, yet not one has asked why it's there. I don't do it on all of them, so if you want to fetch a fly up, all you do is to squeeze the water out of the pad, put a little grease on, and Bob's your uncle.

The nymph patterns tied with seal's fur are naturals for floaters. This is my favourite material for most traditional flies. It may look pretty dead when you have completed the tying and it sits in the vice looking at you, but just add water and it's the most translucent material you would want to see, and used as the dressing for nymphs it's better still. Back to the Pheasant Tail. It's a case of using a fine wire hook and repeating the application of grease, till it does float and it will eventually.

Fish it this way, especially at the end of the season – cast out in a big wind or good ripple and allow it to float in a straight line from rod tip to leader – it will be taken with confidence. The fact that it is still in the water makes no difference because I imagine a fly fished under these circumstances looks as though it is moving because of the surface current washing past it, giving the impression of life. Try a team of the little Black Spiders fished in the same way towards late evening just with the nymphs greased and the leader sunk. They float if tied in the way described for quite a while and when they do eventually sink, retrieve them back slowly in the normal way.

I've already told you about the Orange Seal's Fur Nymph on a flat calm. Try this too in a ripple and also in a range of sizes. The smaller sizes can be deadly at times, not forgetting the Sedge Pupa and Gold Ribbed Hare's Ear, all naturals for this method.

Difficult Conditions

Trying to list what are termed difficult conditions I suppose would differ from angler to angler. The most trying time I find to get fish is when there is a good ripple with the wind coming from the same direction as the sun. And from bitter experience it's the time when I am looking over my shoulder, waiting for the odd cloud in the sky to cover it up. I wait for this, timing my best cast to be in the water and fishing for me the moment the sun is blanked out. I always seem to catch a fish when this happens. I try very often to put myself in the same position as a trout. Due to the surface drift, I should in theory be travelling upwind, picking off all and sundry insects in my path. Looking up to the surface, I am blinded by a myriad of flashes from that great gold ball in the sky reflecting off the ripple. I can't blink because I have not got any eyelids, so to get a little relief I've got to dive down deeper into darker water to get a little shade. So much for fishy thoughts. And of course the answer is to get down deep with a long leader, for I'm a great believer in the buggeration factor. You know, if you drop a slice of bread and jam, it always lands sweet side down, and I know full well that the sun moves over to dodge certain clouds that are on a collision course. However, as I have said, the best odds are to fish deep and by this I mean really deep. It's one of the occasions when I do use a very long leader to be really certain to catch. I've mentioned before that sometimes I use a leader 30ft long.

This raises a question straight away, and I know full well that there are other ways to get deep, such as using a sunk line which for me is not

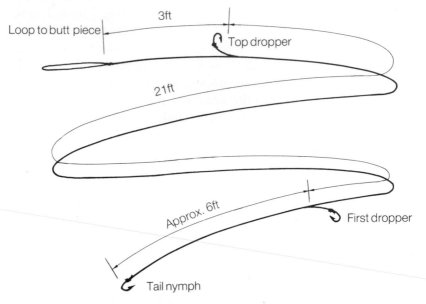

Fig 14   **Assembling long leaders**
If the tail nymph is heavier, the leader will be more
aerodynamic. Level 6lb nylon is usually used. By varying
the length between the droppers, any depth of water can be
fished. This rig is suitable for scraping the bottom in very
deep water (using a floating line). To fish shallower,
shorten leader between the two droppers by cutting out a
piece of nylon between them.

sensitive enough. I usually find that when overhead conditions are
difficult, the fish are the same. The number of fish that take your
offerings into their mouths, only to reject them and not giving any
indication at all to your hand, is, in any case, much more frustrating
than using a long leader.

   The other way is to use a leaded fly and of the two, although I admit I
have not got a great deal of experience with them, they are probably the
best alternative. I've only had a couple of years experimenting with
them on the smaller fisheries and don't consider that this is enough
time to make comment on them. I'll tell you my findings when I get
more use out of them. So I'll stick for the time being to the method I
know.

   The one difficult thing most people I have taught to use the ultra
long leader find is actually getting it started. Don't ever attempt to get it
on the move without at least ten yards of line outside the top ring. The

best and quickest way to achieve this is to pull about four or five yards of line out through the top ring, drop the fly into the water to your right hand side if you are right handed, then moving the tip of the rod from side to side in front of you, to force another five yards outside the tip ring, finishing up with the line lying on the water at the right side. Come straight up into your back cast and extend the line as far as you are able. I find no trouble at all, for the point fly and rest of the leader whips out of the water and with a brisk casting action, follows the path of the line proper. The one thing you must not do is to allow the back cast to drop, and if you have made up your leader as previously described with a breeze at the back or alongside, you will straighten out quite well. From the moment they alight, keep a sharp eye on the end of the line because fishing this method with a long reasonably slow drop, a lot of the takes come while the nymphs are descending. Owing to the drift factor even in water not much above 12ft deep you will rarely touch bottom, but at least you will get down deep enough to get fish, in the majority of the waters in the Midlands. It is a much different story in the limestone lakes of the south where you can actually see the nymph even in 12ft of water most of the time.

The other method of catching fish under these conditions is to go to the other bank and fish into it, for usually a bit of murk stirred up by the wave action can provide the necessary cover that the trout need as long as it is not too muddy.

The next difficult condition that I describe is what is known as preoccupation, or a preoccupied rise. This occurs when you get to the water and sometimes get a couple of fish as they start to move. Then when the water becomes agitated with the rings of rising fish everywhere, although you are covering many more fish than you were before, you fail to make any headway at all. You usually catch another odd fish as the rise abates, then it's time to pack up. I know that most anglers get very frustrated at these times and that always makes matters far worse than they really are. It's even worse to arrive at a water and not see a fish move the whole day, although reputedly well stocked.

To get back to our rise. It does not pay to keep hopping out of the water to change flies until you get the right combination. It does pay to change the presentation of the flies you already have on and, if the fish are close enough, to concentrate on one fish at a time rather than to fish the water. If all the retrieve notes fail, then try the greased up nymph sunk leader method in amongst a lot of fish. This usually works far more often than it fails and if you have done your homework, you should have a team on already that is near enough the mark. One that

Administering the last rites to an early season rainbow.

sometimes works with alarming regularity under these trying times is a Red Spider size fourteen fished stationary. I very rarely fail on a mass rise and I think half the answer is to calm down, think positive and don't blow your mind, and if it's the 'curse', reread what I said before.

Trout fishing is more interesting than any other branch of angling that I know, and even if I live another fifty years, as I expect to, I still will not know it all. There is such a combination of things that can go right or wrong that the answers may possibly need to be worked out with a computer. Consider just a few of the conditions we are likely to meet: weather varying from arctic to red hot with the whole range of temperatures in between including cloud conditions, wind strengths etc, time of year, thousands of insects, bugs, beetles and fish fry, different types of water, depth factor, allied to the numerous types of trout including 'queers', the sexless triploid. It's a wonder we ever get the right combination at all. I think back to the first evening when I really laid into a lot of fish. I thought I'd cracked it, but going back the following evening with the conditions the same, ripple the same, wind in the same direction, overhead conditions the same, fish moving the same, leader and tackle, the flies the same, I fished in the same way. Yes you've guessed it, I never touched a fish. Ah well, back to the drawing board. Sorry, I left one factor out. I used to have an aquaintance at Grafham who, if he caught nothing, used to tell me the barometric conditions were wrong. The fact that I had my whack, and probably a lot of other people too, made no difference to him. I used to think of him like that little boy in the cartoon in one of the daily papers – the one where he usually had his own little cloud over his head. What a load of rubbish, barometric conditions indeed! I can think of far more excuses for not catching salmon than I can think of for trout, including some borrowed from other people. I might write a book of them. Then again thinking of quite a few I've heard, the book would be banned.

Basically the best time to catch trout is when you are at a water with plenty of stock in it, and with your flies in the water. You make your own conditions and this is why, if it is at all possible, I pick a pitch which suits my style of fishing, and if I don't feel at ease I change my spot. I can assure you that there are positions where the wind blows in two directions at once. If you don't believe me, I can take you to a few quite easily. I know all the awkward spots on most reservoirs in the country. How do I know? I've fished 'em. Do not get too serious about it, it's not the end of the world if you don't empty the water of spotted inhabitants at the end of the day. Remember that the ticket you buy is to enable you to fish, it doesn't give you a guarantee to catch fish. Keep it as a sport. Buying a ticket to see a football match doesn't entitle you to come home with Kevin Keegan or Ian Rush under your arm. Once you begin to take this attitude, you are under pressure all the time, and that's no way to enjoy yourself. We are very fortunate nowadays in that most anglers will help rather than hinder, and if the few that do make life a bit difficult would learn the few simple rules of etiquette, things would be a little better.

Allow your neighbour plenty of room and don't creep up on him when he starts to catch. There are usually enough fish in your spot too. By all means ask him what he is using, and far more important, how. To tell the truth, I've found that a lot of people won't believe you in any case.

Good manners cost nothing. And naturally if you know some people very well, it is possible to fish in close proximity. There are probably a dozen friends of mine that I would fish with, actually within a foot, no bother at all, and have done so many times. There used to be a crowd of us who fished a certain bay on Saturday evenings at Grafham. Being a popular fishery in those days, it was invariably crowded at weekends. A few of them would get there a little earlier than most and fish until the rest of us arrived, being mainly shop keepers. The next arrivals got in between them and it used to finish up with about a dozen of us in the space of about sixty or seventy yards of bank. It used to be hilarious and we always, all of us, caught fish.

Bill Poole will remember me falling about when a decent brownie tried and succeeded in tying his legs together. We told him it was safer on the bank. I can remember also one afternoon seeing two boats held together in the middle of the lake and all of a sudden, a squeal of terror from one of them as a certain bloke, who will be nameless, tried to pull a Muddler Minnow from his mate's ear. In the hard bit it was and he finished up going to Huntingdon Hospital to get it removed and still carried on fishing when he returned. What's an ear? I think if they had cut it off he still would have come back for the evening rise. Apprentice surgeons were we all. We must have cost the National Health Service a fortune. The number of blokes with flies stuck in their anatomy was a joy to behold. I remember one chap fishing all day with a lure stuck in his chin, not going to have it out till he got his limit. Seriously though, it does pay to be careful and always wear a good hat and a pair of sunglasses to protect the vulnerable bits.

I once arranged to take one of the old Grafham regulars out in the boat for an evening's fishing. This old chap was an ex-naval comman-der, 'Sailor Bayes' we called him, but not to his face I might add. I got the boat ready in preparation for when he arrived, and took great trouble to get a large ball of clay owing to the lake being flat calm. I stuck it to one side of the central seat as I knew we would need it.

On his arrival, he dashed from the car park, complete with rod and bag, jumped into the boat and I steered off out into the middle of the lake where the fish were moving. Stopping the engine, we both picked up our rods ready to commence, and he sat down after moving to the bow seat, leaned back across the boat towards me, picked up the lump of mud and dropped it over the side. He sat back on his seat and said 'Good. Everything ship shape and Bristol fashion.' As I started the motor up again, I said to him 'It's a good job you were a gun layer and not a diver, or you'd follow that mud to the bottom.'

7 Exact Imitation

When I first started to inspect closely the contents of fish stomachs and attempted to make good copies of the insects found there, I tried to mirror exactly the shape and colours of them. But I rapidly came to the conclusion after a couple of seasons that I was on a very sticky wicket indeed. Achieving an exact imitation is an exciting challenge but the result, no matter how precise, is tested once it is taken out of the vice and presented to the fish. This proved at times most disappointing. I used to put the samples of nymphs and larvae into glass jars and keep the specimen on the table where I would copy them the same in size, shape and colour and be right proud of them too. After attaching them to a length of nylon, I would proceed to drop them into a glass of water with the natural and would compare them with the aid of a magnifier. A lot of the time I used to think to myself, how can they fail?

Thinking back, the one thing I found most difficult was after looking at the 'effort', sitting looking pretty in the vice, and after comparing them in the glass, finding that they went much darker in colour when wet. This was mainly due to the materials I was using at the time which were usually embroidery silks, plus what little fur and feather I could get hold of, which of course limited me severely. Consequently I had to try to allow for this alteration by compensation in using silks of a much lighter shade. Some of them used to look garish and when shown to other anglers, a lot of them used to laugh openly, but I knew more than they, for they looked completely different when wet than sitting snugly in the fly box.

During this period, I managed to borrow a copy of that wonderful book, a classic in its day, John Veniard's *Fly Dresser's Guide*, only to be disappointed in the fact that it listed so few nymphs, one of which I think was a March Brown nymph, which I tied and had a few fish on. However, I learnt much from that book, mainly about materials and how to make the best use of them.

It really showed me the use of seal's fur, in my opinion the most versatile medium of the lot. It is the only one I know that actually looks better in water than out of it and with a little care it can be induced to copy any shape one requires. Even when it looks quite chunky in the vice, it can change into the most translucent image when wet. After using it in conjunction with silks and feathers, I soon appreciated its worth.

The most successful nymphs I now had in my box were the ones incorporating it in the dressing and, stopping to think and looking in my boxes at the end of a very successful season, I came to the conclusion that the ones that did the most damage to the trout were what I would describe as rough impressions of the natural, rather than mere facsimiles of them.

I've read a lot about how trout see things as opposed to humans and quite frankly, don't believe much of it. You will probably be confused with what most biologists call the trout's window and the many anglers who have caught fish by going down to a finer breaking strain in nylon. I can see very fine nylon in my element, why shouldn't trout see it in theirs? I know that there is nothing wrong with a healthy trout's eyesight. Never underestimate what a fish can see because I can assure you that they miss nothing, and if you inspect the contents of some stomachs, you will be surprised at the miniscule size of some of the food that you will find inside, even in quite large fish. Let me assure you that they are not there by accident, for after observing fish at very close range, I find that they take things so small that they are not easily visible to the human eye, and in a lot of instances are less than pinhead size.

That they see nylon is the biggest certainty of the lot, and if they were as intelligent as some would have us believe, then I am also certain we would never catch them at all. The answer must be that they don't connect it with danger until it is too late, allied to the other fact that they may mistake it for strands of weed that are present in the water. Trout can soon become educated, mainly through anglers who proceed to frighten them by continually making a disturbance with bad presentation, and also by unnecessary movement. This is generally borne out by the fact that in very small fisheries where one can actually see the fish, after an hour or so, the inhabitants either go to ground in the weeds or race off as an angler comes into view. They will then only be catchable again after a couple of hours' rest.

They can also become educated to a certain pattern of lure and I can think of times when a lure of a certain colour has been catching fish almost to the point that, if you were to believe many people at the time, it was useless to use another pattern, only to find after a week or so, it failed to produce. Now I do not suppose that every fish in, say, a lake the size of Grafham, has actually seen its mates dragged out after taking this thing. I can only surmise that there is some means of communication between the fish, and it proves how little we know.

That they have many more senses than us is certain. I remember a time at Grafham when eye fluke was present. I caught many very good conditioned fish, which had a white film over both eyes. They took quite small (size twelve) nymphs very readily and I would have said that these fish were blind, but although I was retrieving very slowly, they homed in on the movement.

This must take me back to the copies that we use to fool the trout into believing that what we are offering is what they want to eat. I would suggest that this has got a lot more to do with movement than we realise, or even lack of mobility at times. After long years of trial and error, I have come to the conclusion that shape or profile is important, sometimes exaggerated size, sometimes colour, but most of all movement. The one thing I would stress most of all is the fact that most nymphs when in change from larval to adult stage can go through very drastic changes of colour and form. I suppose that if we look at the finished object, the natural insect sitting on the water, at this stage it may look perfect in every detail while a few seconds before it looked totally different. If you watch a sedge hatching at close range for instance, it appears as a mess, all arms, legs and feelers, and depending on what angle you are looking at, can appear very rough indeed, and go through a colour change you will scarcely believe. Out of all this confusion you must sort out at what stage the trout is going to take it. The sad fact is that quite a few insects when hatching, are not the pretty little things we imagine, and we can use this to our advantage.

Don't get me wrong. I do appreciate a good, well tied imitation of the natural and take my hat off to some of the creations I see on my travels. In a lot of cases they would not be a commercial proposition to tie because most of them would take far too long to produce. To be honest they would not catch as many fish as a rough style offering. I remember starting to fish one evening alongside one of the best, if not the best, innovative fly dressers in the country. I pulled out six fish one after the other and heard him shout along to me 'I thought we were doing well until you came.'

The sad fact is that they look really beautiful in the fly box, but don't seem very good at putting fish on the bank. I will stick to the theory and practice that the impressionist patterns are the most productive. Although the colour ranges of seal's fur are much wider nowadays than they were when I started, I still dye a lot of my own for I find that using a Dylon dye I can take out pieces at different intervals and get a very wide range of shades, especially in the greens and browns, both in seal's fur and feather fibres. One of the most popular feathers of mine for nymph bodies are the wing fibres of a swan or goose, dyed to the appropriate shade.

Going back once again to a few years ago, I have got a 'bock', which I suppose I ought to explain. One of these 'bocks' is a Jonah which means that whenever he appears on the scene, I don't do very well.

I was fishing on my own one freezing afternoon, right up in Savages Creek at Grafham, not a soul in sight, when he appeared coming round the corner. I thought as soon as I saw him, that's it, this is just what I need. (It always seems strange to me that on any large water you may fish, if you are on your own, the very next angler to appear will always come and fish very close to you.)

Strange enough I like this particular bloke immensely. He's very good company and we get on very well and although when he's there my chances of catching fish drop to zero, I don't mind one little bit. Coming up to me, I still concentrating, he gets out his cigarettes, breaks off the filter tip, flicking it into the water in front of me, knowing I don't like fags with spats on, puts it in my mouth and says 'How's it going mate?' Me replying 'No good, and it will get worse now you're here.' (I said before I was blunt), and he laughs and gets in alongside. Well after about another couple of hours, not having seen or felt a fish, I decided if something doesn't happen soon, I'm off. A couple of casts later, I meet with a terrific tug, which by the time it's transferred to my brain, has leapt out of the water, revealing a rainbow about a couple of pounds. I beach it a moment or two later, and my Jonah having some distance to go, clears off, taking the fish with him.

That evening the telephone rang. It was my Jonah's wife, asking me to guess what was in the trout's stomach when she cleaned it. I was surprised when she told me, yes, the filter tip and one white feather. Must have been making itself a feather bed. As I said, it was very cold.

Why more than one Fly on a Leader?

This is a question I am always asked, and the reason I give is not always the one expected, for if I fished with leaders of what is accepted as normal length for me, I find that I cannot straighten them out with a single fly. Now what I consider normal is 18ft long and sometimes even longer and, without going to the trouble of making up a special leader, I can get excellent presentation with no trouble at all.

In the bad old days, leaders were very short and it's only in very recent times that we have been able to buy leaders more than 9ft long. Now one can buy continuous tapered leaders up to 15ft. The only real snag I can see is that when I occasionally get two or three fish on at the same time I have had a limit of eight fish in three casts, ruining my fishing session immediately, for it is possible to limit out too quick. Funnily enough, two or three fish aren't as difficult to handle as one would imagine. They are usually too busy trying to go in opposite directions to worry about where they eventually finish up, and they are high and dry before they realise it, and it's much easier to beach them than use the net.

I don't think a trout makes a selection of the three flies at all and although I am sure it sees them all, most of the time, I've found that a trout will only move so far to intercept a fly. Only on a few occasions, usually when fishing all three close to the surface, have I had the point and first dropper taken by the same fish.

I find that I get more aggro with tangles when fishing a single fly than when I am fishing a team, which I suppose is the opposite to most people's way of thinking. I have yet to lose a fish by going into a weed bed and believe me, I pick the weediest spots through preference. But the real problem I have seen twice is losing a very large fish when on the point fly and having another fish smash into the dropper. I remember in the early days at Grafham, a friend having hooked a fish which he had under control, it was repeatedly diving for the bottom in front of him. He was about twenty yards out in the water and called for help. I told him I'd come out when it was ready and carried on fishing. At the same time I kept a weather eye on him and noticed that his first dropper often dibbled the surface most attractively at times.

This carried on for some minutes and he told me it was a big brownie, so I waded out and picked up his net. I advanced out to within about 10ft of him standing with rod bowed and the dropper still dancing occasionally. All of a sudden another huge fish surfaced 10ft from his dropper and I knew at that moment what was going to happen and, sure enough, it did. That fish, which was a rainbow as far as I could see, about 5lb, surged forward as only a rainbow can. I reckon it was doing about sixty miles per hour when it took with a sickening crack, my friend's rod tip shot skywards and I backed out – I offered him my clean hankie, too.

And I still believe that three flies are better than one, especially from a boat, and I defy anyone to beat me with a single fly against a team. However, don't forget one does not go against the fishery rules and there are some that do stipulate using one fly only. If I felt that strongly about any rules I didn't agree with, I wouldn't go there in any case.

HYBRID TROUT

There have been many experiments trying to cross one type of trout with another and the first one that I can think of was a cross between the brown trout and the rainbow, named the brownbow. This was done in the west country I believe and after a few months was never heard of again, a failure for some reason or another.

The next one I heard of was a cross between brown trout and brook trout, named a tiger trout, supposedly for the ferocity in its fighting qualities. I never met up with one of these so really cannot comment, except to say that if it fights better than a really good conditioned rainbow of 2½lb to 3½lb, then it must be some fish. I don't know of any water where it is stocked.

The next obvious cross tried was the rainbow × brook trout cross, called the cheetah trout and, a few years ago, I did have one of these at Avington. The only difference I noticed was the peculiar spotting arrangement which was like big spots or patches along the sides and once again, do not know of any fishery where they may be caught, apart from Avington.

The brook trout is a beautiful fish which seems to vary in shade of basic colour through the season, starting from bright silver with white spots and white edged fins to a more olive green colour in the larger specimens. Some of the cock fish at the back end of the season have a reddish tinge about them.

I have always wondered about a glass case that used to be in the window of the Midland Northants Water Board office in Wellingborough years ago, which contained three fish, reputedly American brook trout that were taken from Ravensthorpe. They were not the same as the brookies we see today and I remember vividly that the sides of all three had squiggly lines in place of spots and still wonder what variety they were. Looking at Pearson's record, the largest must have pushed it close. I am trying to track this down but it was a long time ago and knowing Water Authorities, it will probably be like banging my head against a brick wall.

The latest addition to the range being tried out is the so-called triploid trout which is a sexless rainbow. By interfering with the genetic arrangements it will not go through the spawning urge and in theory will remain bright and silver through its life, and grow very fast. However I have heard that they are expensive to produce and take longer to breed, which fetches me back to the true rainbow that was stocked into Grafham at the start. I have never seen faster growing fish than those and, accepting the fact that quite a few of them were out of condition, in the second and third seasons during May they soon recovered and were in top nick in June. We never really had that much to complain about and at the time a lot was talked about rainbows and that the cock fish didn't grow as big as the hens. I disagreed with this and still have some pictures to prove that I had male fish over 6lb in very good condition. I'm not against change but God forbid that we have reached a point where we have to 'caponise' fish. I think that it's time we got back to basics and I wonder how recently a fish farm has obtained the true stock from the land of origin. Those original fish grew so fast they looked like bream.

8 Small Waters

Until a few years ago I spent most of my time fishing the larger waters and would never make comment on the smaller waters that were becoming popular. I read with great interest the discussion between a lot of different people, the pros and cons of them, and one of the main points of conflict seemed to be the size of the fish put into some of them. Reports of double figure fish being caught as easy as our twelve inchers on the bigger reservoirs caused quite an amount of controversy. I would not be drawn into it for I knew even then that the fish would soon become educated, even in the big waters. I realised that possibly the conditions in a small water, owing no doubt to angling pressure, would multiply the problems. Even a place like Grafham, for all you have heard about it, did not stay easy for long, and it was mainly in my own case of having quite a lot of experience in lake fishing anyhow that kept me catching fish there. It went terrifically hard for most of the other anglers who only started to trout fish when they heard of the huge catches that could be made there in the opening month or so. Not only the newcomers to trout fishing came unstuck, for I know quite a few of the more experienced men never achieved its full potential either. I felt it rather refreshing to sit on the fence and learnt probably more about small waters in theory from articles and other anglers that made visits to them than any man alive. I found that the ones who caught fish praised them and those who didn't cursed them, which I knew was unfair because those who did not latch onto the big fish available, never did very well on the big reservoirs in any case. It used to disgust me at places like Pitsford to see anglers actually casting at fish while the lorry which had fetched them still had its rear wheels in the water and then proudly boast of catching their limits. I would say nothing if they were beginners and would have put it down to ignorance, but quite a lot of them were very experienced men indeed and in my opinion there was no excuse for actions of this kind. I do realise that anyone can catch 'stockies' by accident, but to go deliberately for them is unforgivable, and, as anyone who eats trout will tell you, they taste horrible and improve greatly in both taste and colour after being in the wild for a month or so.

The first small water I ever fished was a very small pond that a local farmer had stocked some six years before. He stopped me as I was driving past one day and asked me if I would catch some of the large trout as he wanted to restock it and was afraid that the large fish would eat them. I enquired of him if they were brown trout and he said 'No, they're rainbows,' and I said I doubted if any would still be alive after six years. He just smiled and said 'It's full of them, but they're not easy to get.' The following evening I got there and putting on a Pheasant Tail, chucked it in, let it settle, started to retrieve and it had not moved a foot before it was stopped as though I had stuck in the bottom. I felt a wriggle, put some pressure on and the fish, for that's what it was, took off and after a lot of hard pulling, I landed a rainbow just under 10lb and upon recommencing, could not catch another fish on it. Fish after fish followed it but take it they would not. I put on in its place an Orange Nymph, to have this taken by another fish, 7lb, and once again many follows, but no takes. After changing again, this time to a size ten longshank Gold Ribbed Hare's Ear, I was lucky enough to get two fish in successive casts, one 8lb, one 5½lb and from then on once again I had fish following all the way to the lift off. I changed the fly to a size eight Corixa and got my last fish, just 3½lb. I will never cease to wonder why I had to change the fly to get another fish. Had every fish seen the original fly and seen their companions in dire straits?

I happened to mention this to Alan Pearson, and he said that at Avington lakes in Hampshire, he sometimes has to do the same and finds that, once having a fish, if he puts it over another fish, very often they refuse it and the change of fly sometimes works.

Another thing I found strange was the fact that these trout had lived in this pond for six years. It is usually accepted that they only live about four years but all were in very good shape. Although not as bright as new pins they were all acceptable. The smallest fish, a cock, was the darkest but still a nice shape. I wonder now whether they live as long in our larger waters?

The next small fishery I went to was Church Hill Farm at Mursley, near Bletchley and although I had heard a lot about it from quite a few people, all favourable, I was very surprised to find that it was quite a bit larger than I had imagined, comprising two lakes in the most beautiful surroundings, set in a valley below an old farmhouse with a magnificent clubhouse and shop, with terrific lunches and wine.

The fishery comprises two lakes, Dogleg which is the smaller of the two, roughly of a triangular shape, and Jubilee which is separated from its partner by a dam. The one thing which strikes me most is that although only a few yards apart they actually fish completely differently.

Dogleg I would estimate is about three acres and is fed by a stream which, looking from the clubhouse, comes in from the left hand corner, and usually is extremely clear, more so than the larger lake. Although it has quite an area of deep water towards the dam end, most of the other end is shallow and the stream bed holds a fair amount of fish. They can often be seen in this shallow area and I must admit that nothing pleases me more than to creep around this area, casting to a fish I can see. At times the fish seem to rise more freely in this lake which has its devotees who much prefer it to the larger lake. However, when the fish rise in Jubilee, it's a sight to behold. The size of some of them is awesome and it's well known by quite a few of the regulars that there are brown trout in here well into double figures. Rainbows of the same ilk will also

Playing a fish on Jubilee Lake, Church Hill Farm.

appear from the deeps to tantalise you at your feet.

On my first visit there, I remember a chap fishing in the corner of the dam using a sunk line and lure for an hour or so. He suddenly stopped and with rod well bent, said to me that he was stuck in the bottom. I, having, as I said, watched him for some time, noticed that he was waiting a considerable time to get it down deep, replied 'You don't seem to have caught on the bottom before. Be careful, it may be a fish,' and he, pointing his rod down the line, pulled, only to have the bottom move and was smashed instantly. The one thing I have learnt is to treat every stoppage with suspicion, for a large fish can take your offering and sit for a while before deciding to take off. And one other fortunate thing happened on this first visit in that I met Alan Pearson and his mate John Cronin (a detective constable from Bletchley). Having no leaded flies at all, Alan promptly got out his collection and gave some to me with some good advice on how to use them. Of course he helped himself to a fair selection of mine also. Thinking back I recollect the most sound advice of all was when he told me to fish right up to bank. Many of these fish get very educated within a day or two of being stocked and if they remain in the water, probably know more than we do, and will follow your offering to the moment of lift off. Yes Alan, I know now it pays to dangle at the last moment, and it really paid off for me.

However, sometimes those leaded flies come in very handy, but more often than not you can use your normal nymphs and bugs. I always wonder why a lot of anglers associate big lures with the larger fish as both of these guys use small nymphs with great success, especially John Cronin. I think he knows this water better than most and I'm not too proud to take advice from anyone who knows what he's talking about.

This fishery is well worth a visit for once going there, you won't be able to keep away. It's the most civilised place I know and one of the very few places I can relax, sometimes only to sit and watch is a real pleasure. It has a minimum of rules and, always well stocked, some-times easy, sometimes not. The one thing I am certain of is you will always see plenty of fish and enjoy yourself for the place is very friendly, a credit to Tim and Don the owners. A fishery where you can either stalk a 'biggy' or fish the water.

Soon after visiting Church Hill Farm I went to the Avington Fishery of Sam Holland's down in Hampshire. Once again having heard much about it and the huge size of some of the fish from there, I prepared myself a little better. This time I had at least tied a half dozen leaded

Gin-clear water at Avington makes it possible for Bob Church to
spot fish for a fellow angler.

flies to add to the selection given me by Pearson. On arrival I was very
impressed by what I saw for there was a stock pond full up with fish,
some in excess of 18lb and the majority well into double figures. The
biggest help I had was from Roy Ward the manager, for he pointed out
to me the fact that in this gin clear chalk water, the fish appear to be
much smaller than they really are. Not much later I found out how true
this was, for after going up to the top lake with my companions, all
experienced with this water, I watched one of them in a very few
minutes stalk and successfully land a fish of 11lb. After having seen a
film some time before of a couple of 'notabilities' fishing the same lake
and at the same time thinking they could do with a casting lesson, I
inspected the fish and more so the nymph he had used. I then began to
understand why the casting looked so rough, for the nymph was so
heavy. Those I had tied were lightweights compared with it.

    I knew straight away that I was undergunned and was taken a little
down the bank to find a fish. On being asked what size did I think it was

At Avington, using a peach-coloured line!

and how deep, remember saying about 8lb, 6ft down and was instantly corrected by being told about 14lb plus at 10ft deep. The water was so clear you could see every spot on it and I was told to have a go at it which I declined, saying I would go and find my own. I walked quietly up to the top of the lake which is the narrowest of the three, and tried to make myself inconspicuous by crouching down behind the bankside reeds with a patch of submerged weeds just over the half way mark. After a few minutes' wait, a fish came slowly along and swam behind this weed bed and I, having replaced my own nymph now with a real heavy Mayfly Nymph, one that Pearson had given me, dropped it to the far side watching it sink in line with the direction the fish was going. I remember thinking to myself what a horrible splash that thing made as it 'hit' the water, the impetus of it actually dragging the fly line forward smartly across the top as the leader straightened. I watched it sinking much slower than I thought it would, to see the fish suddenly appear from its cover and swim over to my very obvious morsel, open its great white mouth, and I instantly lifted. I saw the nymph come up, no connection at all, and the fish carried on slowly to my left as though nothing had happened. That the fish had had the nymph in its mouth I was certain, so feeling rather bemused I let the whole lot drop back and watched it sink once more. I could see it the whole time and after a few minutes saw another fish coming in the same direction as before, only this one looked about 5lb and once again it disappeared behind the weed bed. I pulled a couple of handfuls of line to cast into the same place as before. I didn't get that far though for on the second pull and lifting the rod in preparation to laying the ambush, my rod lurched downwards with a sickening jar and in a great silver flash a fish had appeared from nowhere and had swallowed the nymph out of sight. It didn't seem to like it one bit for it instantly whipped about twelve yards of line out and was now trying to make a hole in the other bank which I didn't like much either. Putting all the pressure on I could, I pulled it out into the open water where I got more or less on even terms with it and after a struggle, managed eventually to slip the net under it. A nice fish of 9½lb. I told you before I was lucky.

I hadn't seen that fish at all, it just must have crept along the bank under my feet and from then on I decided to try to look more closely. On creeping up the bank, I found another which this time worked out as planned for I managed to drop the lump of lead about ten feet in front of it and as it sank to its level, the fish obligingly tipped up to meet it. Its great white mouth opened and when it shut, I lifted to be met with a solid downward pull and I was in another fish – 6lb. I never had one of

Unhooking a rainbow taken on a Pheasant Tail Nymph from Linch Hill Lake.

the double figure fish but enjoyed myself immensely, mainly watching the experts and learning much more about these clear water lakes. If I remember correctly, there were seven fish over the 10lb mark, the best fish taken by John Cronin, over 15lb. I finished up with four fish and was much wiser when I left than when I started – you're never too old to learn at this game. I'll be back there too.

Another of the smaller fisheries I like is the Black Monk Trout Lakes at Lenchwick near Evesham, Worcestershire. Once again this is a twin lake complex, set in beautiful surroundings with nice clear water, well stocked with good quality fish that are always in tip top condition. This is a lake where one can either stalk biggies or fish the water and again expect to run into double figure fish as there are plenty. It's owned and run by a very amiable character by the name of Hywel Morgan with a minimum of rules and a friendly atmosphere. Very good fishing with small nymphs and pupae and free rising fish – a joy to be there.

The last but not least of the smaller waters that I fish is my home water of Ringstead Grange, a rather larger water than the others, being roughly of a square shape of 36 acres or so. It is very well stocked with browns, rainbows, brookies and salmon at no extra cost. When you catch a salmon it's counted in your limit as a trout. Owned and run by Harold Foster, this fishery is well stocked with fish of all sizes. They are very free rising fish and one can use all the techniques available though I find nymphs of all shapes and sizes to be successful and take a lot of fish on the dry fly.

The list of big fish is impressive and it's not many days that it does not yield fish between 5 and 16lb. As I said, it also now has salmon stocked and I know that it is the only lake where this has been done successfully at the moment. I personally have had only three, one on a size twelve Black Spider, the other two on Corixas. Although when the first stocking was done, lures caught a fair few of them with anglers getting two each towards their limits, a very nice bonus indeed. It has produced rainbows over 16lb, brownies to just under 10lb, although I have seen a few of them up to 14lb. One was hooked, lost and found dead at this weight. There are also a few brookies over 4lb. All the fish seem to prosper in here owing no doubt to the clear clean water. This is a place where it pays to expect the unexpected for I often get quite big fish on small nymphs and bugs. My favourite flies for this water are the Black Spiders, Corixa and Sedge Pupa and occasionally the Grey Pheasant Tail, not forgetting when fishing dry, the Grey Buzzer, Wickham's Fancy and in season, the Daddy Longlegs.

With a rainbow limit at Black Monk.

Ringstead.

Like all the previous waters mentioned, the smaller fisheries seem to have a much more club like clientele who are very friendly and helpful. Strangers are made welcome on them as long as they behave themselves and this usually pays dividends because once they know you are straight, the help can be very much to your advantage.

All in all, I can only say that I am still learning to fish the small waters myself and although generally very successful, owing perhaps to experience, I realise I still have a long way to go, for on the larger waters I can usually forecast what is going to happen and know how to overcome most of the problems. It seems to me that these fish sometimes have their own ideas for the longer they are in a water, the more difficult they are to catch, so I must deduce that they get more educated every day. This is just the same in the bigger waters. The idiots are always caught first. I do not purposely hunt for big fish as I firmly believe the most sporting fish to catch is a rainbow between $2\frac{1}{2}$ and $3\frac{1}{2}$lb and these are definitely the ones that will give you the most trouble to land. The fact is if you are fishing somewhere near right, you will pick up, as I do, more than your fair share of the larger specimens.

The fish in the smaller waters probably see more different flies in an hour than fish in the waters like Grafham and Rutland see in a month, and the less disturbance you make either by standing over fish or bad presentation, the more your chances are improved.

9 Large Waters

Eyebrook

Our early trips to Eyebrook were the real beginning to the art of reservoir fishing, and the education I had there has stood me in good stead ever since. This water was stocked to attract workers to the Stewart & Lloyds steelworks from north of the border and was made and landscaped to look as much like a Scottish loch as possible. It was stocked with brown trout only, for in those days, as far as we were concerned, rainbows were not known of locally but we had heard of them when reading about Blagdon lake. The wonderful record fish of 8lb 8oz, caught by Lt Col Creagh-Scott in 1924 had stood for a good many years and in passing, I wonder what that gentleman would think now of the huge fish I have seen in fish farms of over 30lb.

The rules were different in those days and one was allowed to spin from the dam and one hundred yards from the bank in a boat, and on the first couple of visits, I took a very light spinning rod which after a few casts was discarded and never taken again. The fly is the deadliest way to catch trout and if you read back in trout fishing history, you will learn that the professional trout fishermen who sold their fish to the hotels and markets used the fly rod in the main.

And the most important thing that I learnt during this stage was etiquette, the basic good manners of conduct both on the bank and in boat fishing. Woe betide any who broke them at this water for they soon knew about it. Mr Robinson, the manager of this water, never missed a move by any angler there, and even if you rowed across in front of a drifting boat at a distance of a hundred yards, you soon got to know about it. You never went within thirty yards of another angler on the bank and never fished anywhere near another man without first asking permission. If passing behind somebody already fishing, you let them know audibly and told them when you were clear. This lesson could be taken by a lot of people nowadays, for I have had, while knocking fish on the head, a boat actually anchoring in my pitch while bank fishing at Grafham. It was so close, only a couple of yards out, that I picked up his anchor and putting the anchor into it, pushed the boat out physically. I only incurred Mr Robinson's displeasure once, and that was an

Eyebrook Reservoir is one of the waters where I learnt the tricks of the trade. This photograph shows it at low level during a summer drought.

occasion when in high summer, fishing with a few friends late one evening, I decided to fish a little later than usual owing to the conditions. The rise never occurred until it was nearly dark and I fished on, only to see his car come across the dam. Ignoring everyone else, he stopped immediately behind me and said politely 'It's time you signed out Mr Cove,' jumped in his car and drove off. I apologised to him and later on in the pub, one of my mates said 'I wonder why he picked on you' and I knew the answer to that too. After the number of years I had fished there I knew the rules better than anyone else present and should have set the example. He was the most kindly man I ever met and many is the person he helped by supplying rods, waders and equipment forgotten in the rush to get there. I knew him for thirty years and never ever called him by his Christian name and I was very sad when he died. He taught and inspired me more than he ever knew. A man everybody respected and, if he ever did have a reason to tell somebody the error of their ways, it was done by being taken to one side, and most politely. I will never forget him – a gentleman.

That this water held a lot of big fish at the time was well known and nearly every week there were fish between five and eight pounds taken, mainly on small flies for not many people used lures in those days. It was stocked with rainbows later on and, although pressure on the lake increased, it was still a good water to fish. In my opinion it is a far better brownie water, for rainbows don't seem to get too big in there. I always said if you could learn to fish Eyebrook successfully, you could catch fish anywhere, and to an extent it's still true, for I served my apprenticeship well and it was a hard school for me, being self taught in every branch of casting, presentation, fly tying and basic entomology. Apart from odd trips to Ravensthorpe and Hollowell, I spent most of my free hours there.

Chew Valley and Blagdon

Once we heard about Chew Valley opening, we started to go down there quite often and this, together with Blagdon, although quite a distance from home, provided a lot of experience in landing better quality fish. It was at both of these venues that we met up with the bigger rainbows which in my opinion were a much harder fighting fish. I remember the first one I had, a fish of just under 3lb that stood on its tail at me and scorched off about thirty yards of backing in no time at all. It was trouble all the way to the bank. The brownies, once having their first rush, will tend to fight deep and steady, and can be subdued at a leisurely rate. But this new fish, after fetching it into the shallows, instantly turned round and took another thirty yards of line out in a flash. I thought the fight was as near to a sea trout in a lake as we would ever get and I became very keen about catching them.

Pitsford

It was a few more years before Pitsford opened and we had them a little closer to home. Before Pitsford was opened, I did quite a lot of research into the lie of the land. This was to pay dividends later in the fact that I knew where the ditches and streams that traversed it were and with this knowledge, I started to take my toll of the fish consistently, although it was never very heavily stocked. I will never be able to understand why the Midland Northants Water Board made a big error in not doing a proper job in making this water the Mecca for trout fishermen for, in my opinion, this lake caused the true explosion in trout fishing, not

As Arthur Cove likes it best, perfect calm conditions at Chew Valley.

Grafham which opened some years later, for it attracted anglers from quite a wide area. Being close to Northampton and within easy driving distance of Leicester, Coventry, Birmingham and London, it attracted quite a large crowd on most weekends and a lot of the successful anglers today both locally and from more distant climes cut their teeth on it. It seems to produce both good rainbows and browns. The latter breed successfully in the feeder streams which in the lean years provide quite a stock of natural born fish. In the last couple of years it has been stocked more realistically and provides much more sport than hitherto. Most people used to desert it after about the end of June and it was possible to have a lot of bank to oneself. This is one of the larger waters that has the most free rising fish of the lot from both bank and boat and a team of small flies or nymphs will more often than not prove this. I know that it holds more than its fair share of big brownies, which quite a few of the local anglers with their superior knowledge take toll of. Its shape gives it plenty of bank space with nice little bays and points where it is possible to do your own thing without too much disturbance. The one queer thing about Pitsford is that I have never seen or heard of anyone ever catching a pike, although there is quite a head of coarse fish netted out from time to time.

Grafham

A few years after Pitsford opened, I heard that another large reservoir was planned at Diddington, and when construction started, I made it my business to spend a lot of time exploring the valley which was dammed to cause, as it was later named, Grafham Water. Once it started to get water in it, I watched and waited as the first stock of trout went in as small fish even before the dam was completed, and they just grew so fast it was unbelievable. When it was nearly full I used to drive down the road at Hill Farm that disappeared under the water and park the car and watch the numerous fish in excess of 4lb swimming close in to the bank. I waited patiently for it to open, which it did on the 1st July 1966, and finished on 30th September with the result of 10,167 fish being taken. By far the bigger number were between the 2lb to 5lb mark, 7,383, with some 401 fish over this weight, up to 8lb, impressive to say the least. This was after only three months and it was possible in the first weeks to fish by oneself in places like Savages Creek and the west bank for the news had not got around. But after this it gradually got more crowded as more and more arrived to reap the harvest.

How those fish fought, believe me, you certainly needed a hundred yards of backing on the reel for I have never had fish run so hard and fast as those early Grafham fish. The number of times anglers were broken, even on 10lb leaders, was unbelievable. It was possible to have it snapped without even knowing it had happened. I am of the opinion that those fish were of a special breed for I've never had fish so fast and violent since. They seem to have less fight as the years progress. There must be a reason for this, and I wonder if the strain of rainbows we have in the country at present are so inbred that they have lost this vastly superior quality. To be honest I've never had even large salmon in rivers attempt to put anywhere near the same distance between me and

One of a fine bag of eight caught by Arthur Cove whilst out on Grafham with Bob Church.

them as those fish. Everyone you speak to who fished at that time agrees that this was so, and I used to think that because they were put in and had in the main a complete season or so to grow naturally, they had reverted back to the wild. But even this theory was proved wrong to me after experiences on other waters stocked in the same way; that they were something special is true and the next season, 1967, the fish were more or less evenly distributed throughout the months, averaging just over five thousand, finishing with 32,029 fish, not bad going by any means.

Although the fishing was getting harder, the number of anglers there had to be seen to be believed. If anyone had told me that I would have to go and queue the night before an opening day, I wouldn't have thought it possible. The following season, 1968, the bulk of the fish were caught in the early part of the season, and from then on most anglers struggled. It was nothing to do with a lack of fish for I was getting plenty although it was a cold wet summer – if you fished right they were there to be caught. This is the time when my nymph fishing tactics came to the fore and often, fishing alongside more experienced men, I was the only one taking fish. So much so that I could give a written guarantee to get them, for with the knowledge I had, I knew certain spots that always produced fish. Owing to certain conditions, wind drift, food availability, and so on, at certain times fish lived in these spots and could always be caught. Even when I couldn't get into a more preferred spot, I still caught fish. Although in the previous two seasons big lures pulled fast through the water produced most of the fish, many anglers were not prepared to try anything else and suffered accordingly, and even in this, the most difficult season so far on this great water, I never blanked at all. A lot of the time, owing to pressure of business, I was confined to an hour or so in the evening. The bulk of the food in their stomachs was still snails and sometimes leeches which were quite predominant in the water, so much so that the sticks of the sunken hedges were covered in them. These spots could produce a much better than average sized fish. I remember one limit bag I made during this season of eight fish for 52½lb. The other main source of food visible at this time was the vast number of sticklebacks that had multiplied by now and, when wading, came in the shade of your body to shelter from both sun and the marauding trout that scattered them from between your legs. About this time, Richard Walker devised the Polystickle lure to catch these sticklebacks, and very effective it was too.

A good Grafham rainbow falls to a Pheasant Tail Nymph.

BROWNS, RAINBOWS AND BROOKIES

I think the other thing I learnt about at this time was the difference between the brown trout and the rainbow fish. They are of vastly different temperaments. Most of the fish were large enough to see quite clearly and their reactions in the main to both movement and presentation were totally different. I rapidly realised that rainbows tended to travel in shoals. That learnt, I attempted to get them in as fast as possible and despatch them while still standing in the water, and get my nymphs out again. In this way I would sometimes be able to get three of them while they were in the area, before they moved off. The lack of disturbance I caused by not (as most anglers did) going to the bank to despatch them and then wading back out gave me a ratio of three to one over other anglers. I also learnt that when one was standing still the fish would swim quite close, while any movement would make them swim quickly out of the area. So I would take the trout closest to me, sometimes within feet of me, so as not to disturb the main shoal. I never could understand why most people ignore a fish at their feet. If you do everything slow and easy they are all catchable. The moment you attempt to cover a fish further away and 'line' a fish close to you, the

A mixed bag from Rutland.

near one bolts and the rest get the message. It's not long before you are fishing blank water and waiting for the next shoal to arrive.

When a brownie turns up, sometimes a loner or sometimes in a shoal, they will often know you are there and will continue feeding even though you put offerings in front of them repeatedly. Unless you do something stupid they will stay within close proximity for a fair length of time, taking all and sundry except what you have tied to the leader. The best thing you can do with these is to give them a rest for five minutes after a couple of casts, or wait till you get a slight change in conditions. A puff of wind can make all the difference, and presented right, a fly will usually be taken as though that is what was wanted all the time.

I wonder how many people have noticed that when playing a rainbow it never, to my way of thinking, actually looks at you. Although fighting furiously, it is never really conscious that you are there. How different the brown trout, which seems to keep its eye on you all the time. Maybe it's just the impression I get, but I feel sure this is so.

Brook trout, an addition to some waters I fish, are another variety that take some understanding, and most people say that they are not suited to a lot of waters. But I have found that when first stocked, they are quite easy to catch. They then tend to disappear and are not usually seen again. My experience at Ringstead in the first part is true but in the last three seasons they have reappeared in the shallows at the back end of the season, greatly increased in size. They usually take quite easily and I have seen a few caught there over 4lb apiece.

There is a hell of a lot we don't know about trout and one of the problems is black fish. Now it is generally accepted that rainbows go black at spawning time and to an extent this is true, especially as far as the cock fish are concerned. But, sometimes when moved from the stock pond, where they have been observed to be bright healthy fish, to a new environment, a lot of them go dark, and not only the cock fish either. Now when I ask the supplier to explain this, the answer is usually 'stress' and although I agree that this could be the case, why doesn't it happen every time? Sometimes it makes no difference at all, and if they don't know, it is about time somebody found the answer. And they don't need to be moved a long way either because often this will happen to fish held in a net in the same water that they are released in.

Getting back to Grafham though, I remember the number of complaints once voiced about the fish there. The main one was short rising and fish following and not taking. I did not find this so, for

Any fish of around two pounds is a good one. This rainbow came
from Linch Hill.

generally fishing at this time slow and deep with either the big Pheasant Tail or the Red Diddy, the takes were so slow and confident that I could not miss them if I tried. I wondered if it was due to the trout getting educated to the fact that anything moving fast was to be treated with suspicion and rejected. I still believe that a trout is so quick that so-called short rising is a figment of the imagination and that the trout has had the fly in its mouth and rejected it as a wrong 'un without you being aware that it has actually tasted it. I remember being asked to take out a gentleman and his son for a day's boat fishing. As far as I can remember he was a chemist from Saffron Walden. He, having just come back from a few days at Chew Valley, fished his flies quite fast in the flat calm on that day. I demonstrated how the slow, deeper retrieve with the Pheasant Tail nymph was far more effective by putting eight fish in the boat in short time. Now this goes to show really how one lake differs from another in that I knew that if I had been fishing Chew at this time, I too would have retrieved fast.

One of the significant things at this time, except for a few isolated instances, was the lack of weed growth around the bank which normally would have become established in the three or four years that had passed since opening. I could not really understand why the weeds had not grown. It should have been fairly obvious really; for no doubt it was the amount of wading that was done. I noticed that the areas where there was some weed were the places that were furthest away from the car parks. The only places it grew in any quantity were Savages Creek and the west bank, both of which one had to tramp quite a long way to get to. It paid dividends to fish among this weed for I caught a lot of good fish in the Creek that back end, mainly browns in the 5 to 8lb class.

The following year pike became a problem and, although the water authority were a bit slow in combating them, they eventually got on top of them by netting and trapping. That they were in there from the start is true, as the brook that runs in from Savages Creek was known locally as the Jack Brook and was never thoroughly cleared of them before stocking. That being said, Grafham, although not a beautiful fishery (and I think much could be done with landscaping, especially in front of the Yacht Club which looks worse than a caravan park), still has the potential and continues to produce very good fish. It seems it has its highs and lows, as many other fisheries, but with good management it should continue as one of our leading trout waters. The man who was responsible for most of the hard work that was put in during a number of years has retired recently. Major Fleming-Jones did a very good job.

I have no complaints at all – it is still a top class water that has never treated me badly at all – like all the other places I fish. If you used your 'loaf' the fish did the rest.

Even small fish have big mouths.

Rutland Water

Another large reservoir started to be built and I definitely did my homework on this one, for it is the largest man-made lake in Europe. I was fortunate enough to get a map long before it started and trod a lot of the ground before it was flooded to provide a surface area of 3,100 acres when full. Owing to a bad drought which exposed most of the other reservoirs' bare bottoms in the year previous to its opening, it enabled me to do a lot of research into the food available. I was pleased to find an abundance of snails, millions of earthworms, chironomids and two types of leeches. The black one features a lot in trout's diet and there was a light coloured buff one which I hadn't seen before. I also found freshwater shrimps, Cinnamon and Silverhorn sedges, plus, to my great surprise, a few of the great red sedges, your actual Irish 'Murraghs'. Damsel flies and olives plus the usual collection of water beetles, including my old favourite corixa were there, and I observed a multitude of fish mainly in the $1\frac{1}{2}$ to 2lb range. I presume that these were the original stocking of 360,000 rainbows put in during March the year before (1975). Then the authority took the chance of putting in fry size browns, 54,000, plus 170,000 rainbow fry as was stated at the time. They were fifty to the pound, very small fry indeed. It was also stated that the level of the reservoir covered 2,500 acres, low because of the previous year's drought. If we take their word (not counting predation of the very small fish that had been stocked), 620,000 were put in, giving an average of 248 fish per acre – quite a high average if the fish were evenly spread. I waited with anticipation for the opening day and decided not to fish but to have a walk round and get a truer picture of what was happening. I'm glad I did, for as I expected, it was bedlam. I think every trout fisherman in the country was there (it seemed so anyway), and walking from Barnsdale towards the lodge at Whitwell, I saw plenty of fish between 1½ and 2lb being caught. The majority were in beautiful condition, especially the browns, but what disturbed me the most was seeing grown men using fisticuffs, fighting because they couldn't get the pitch they wanted, even to the extent that the police were called down to the bank. Sportsmen? I'd personally have shot them. Of course this was hushed up at the time and I know it disgusted a lot of the other anglers present, so much so that a couple of chaps I saw going back to their cars told me, 'We are going to our home water where we know we can fish in peace.' By all accounts it was alright when they started, they being about twenty yards apart. Then more anglers came and got in between them and were actually casting over their lines. What a performance! I always thought fishing was a peaceful recreation!

I inspected the stomachs of quite a few fish that morning and the majority of them were packed full of earthworms, great big balls of them, and it was fairly obvious that as the lake slowly filled, it was forcing these out of the soil and the fish were taking full advantage of this nutritious food source. The average I saw was about 2lb with the occasional rainbow of 3lb, which I considered very good under the circumstances. I decided to leave it alone for a few months, for at this time most of the anglers had deserted Grafham and in my opinion the fishing was better there anyway. On going back there in late August with a friend for an evening's trial, I decided to fish the Normanton bank which was still crowded. We had to walk from the car park towards the dam, passing a line of anglers, in most cases wading up to the crutch, till I came to the end of the line. There was a gap of about a hundred yards between these and the other line of fishermen that had come in from the dam end. I tackled up, my friend having stopped to talk about fifty yards back. I put a Pheasant Tail on the point and two

Black Pupae on the droppers, muddied the leader and stood looking for the signs, which I soon saw. A fish moved in the very shallow water within a yard of the bank about ten yards away, and I dropped the leader about 6ft outside it. On the first pull I lifted into a brown trout just over 2lb. With rod bent in two, my friend walked towards me and laughingly said 'I was going to tell you it's not easy.' When I landed it I found, as expected, that it was cram full of worms. To cut a long story short, both my friend and I walked back to the car within an hour and a half, with our limits. I enquired of every angler, some forty of them between where we fished and the church, and the most that one angler had caught was four fish and he had fished since lunch time. I'm sure that most of the fish were behind them. We never even got our wellies wet – there's a lesson for you. Rutland Water is a beautiful place and there was plenty of scope to get out of the way once it had steadied down a bit. The following season I moved into the locality, and over the next couple of seasons fished every inch of it from both bank and boat.

The second season proved to be better in that the fish improved rapidly in size and it was not long before it was producing fish, both browns and rainbows, over 4lb, with increasing regularity. However it was not in most pitches easy water, and I soon found that like Grafham, certain spots held fish all the time while others produced nothing or very little. There were certain lovely pieces of bank that, after trials over a long period, produced only the odd fish or none. I felt sorry for a stranger to the water, arriving and having no idea where the bulk of the fish were. He would usually have a trying time.

That said, I worked out that the more experienced and dedicated anglers were still getting the bulk of the fish, and, the same as the opening season, usually the better quality fish as well. There are few anglers who can adapt from water to water and possibly the sheer size of Rutland put them off in any case. Now I fish some loughs in Ireland which you could drop Rutland into and lose, but the locations of fish are basically the same. They will frequent the places where most food is available and where it is reasonably quiet. Of course the fish in the Midland reservoirs are stocked as opposed to naturally restocked as in the Irish water. The pressure is much greater on the fish here, due no doubt to sheer numbers of fishermen. Very few anglers fish from the bank in Ireland and it was well known that a large number of fish had retreated to the vast amount of bank allocated to the nature reserve. The only anglers who could take a real advantage of this were the boat fishermen. They would tell us that in these areas the fish were often close into the banks. I think that the policy of pandering to conservationists to such an extent is a bad thing, for I've yet to see other anglers disturb birds, or birds be frightened of anglers. Bird watchers are the only people I have seen lift birds off the nest at Grafham to photograph the nest. I know that there are more birds' nests in the areas available to anglers at Grafham than on the west bank which is preserved most of the season. Fish are not daft, once they have survived the initial onslaught of being stocked, they soon learn where these quiet places are, and who can blame them for taking advantage of this?

I know this to be true, for at Pitsford when the part of the reservoir closest to the dam at the yacht station end was closed off to fishermen, many chaps used to jump over the wire after the bailiff had been round in the evening. Only a few yards into the reserve they caught fish instantly while other anglers on the legal side of the fence struggled.

A lot of anglers struggled at Rutland and, rather than blame their own techniques, they blamed the fishery and this was not fair. I can blame them for allowing lead lining and a few other things that I don't agree with, but that the fish were there and catchable was certain – as proved by myself and a lot of other men. If you learnt the lesson that certain spots always held fish, they were not hard at all for if you fished spots where they had none of the normal pressures, they responded immediately.

A typical example of this was on the Hambleton peninsular. The spots where the water flooded into the trees in a series of bays produced many good fish for me. I found that owing to the branches, you couldn't get a long line out and many was the fish caught within a few yards of the bank. I certainly never saw another angler fishing in these places, and they never saw me for I used to park my car and walk well away from it. Even this dodge developed a pattern for sometimes I would get a limit on the first evening, sometimes another on the second. Then I would have to move to the next bay the following evening, getting fish easily once more. I got the impression that I decimated the population in places which were usually taken up by new residents within a week or so. Most of these fish were good brown trout with the occasional rainbow, the average size of the fish for me were four pounders. Towards the back end of the second season, the fish went mad on the Burleigh Shallows, mainly consisting of good brownies up to $4\frac{1}{2}$lb. I had no complaints at all, and to impress the importance of cover and camouflage, I remember being rebuked once by another angler on the north side of the peninsular one evening from the stones on a corner there, when he remarked about me wearing a white sweater. When he was asked what colour the stones were, he said 'white'. I still don't think the penny dropped.

It has continued to produce a lot of good fish although, in my personal opinion, the stocking rate is not high enough for a water of this size. From what I gather, the hatchery has never come up to expectations, for there was talk at one time of it being able to breed enough fish for all the Anglia Water Authority waters. I hear it does not supply enough fish to stock Rutland alone and firmly believe that if enough attention was paid to the feeders, possibly there could be a natural influx of brownies to create a supply of fish that cost nothing. There is no doubt that the brown trout do very well in there. Possibly reintroducing mayfly which used to abound in the river that ran through the valley would help. Rutland Water is the most scenic reservoir I have ever fished in the most convivial countryside you will ever see.

Bewl Bridge

Though this water is not a Midland reservoir, being situated on the Kent-Sussex border and being of some 770 acres, I have on quite a few occasions visited it and have found it to be another very good fishery. In my opinion it is probably the best stocked large water in the country. If anyone asked me, I always used to say it's half water, half fish. On my first few visits I found it a waste of time because it only used to take a dozen casts to get a limit of six fish. The rules were that every fish had to be killed regardless of size, so it was hardly worthwhile driving from home through London, a journey there and back of some six to seven hours depending on traffic, to have your whack within minutes. At least you can now buy another ticket (which you couldn't do then) and if I lived in London or south of it, I would fish it far more often as it contains many fish of good size. In its first season it produced a total catch in excess of 48,000 fish, some 8,000 more than mighty Rutland. There is a lack of access roads, which in my opinion is a good thing, for if you are prepared to walk, it's possible to get away from the crowds and find yourself a nice quiet spot – well worth the trouble. I see a bright future for this water as it contains very good sized fish, both browns and rainbows, and once again, very nice scenery and a very helpful staff.

10 Chironomids, Other Insects and Imitations

The one thing that never ceases to interest me is the fact that we know so little about the insects we try to copy in our never ending search to fool the fish. There are, according to the books I have read, 26 genera and over 380 species of chironomids. Most books cover the whole range in a half dozen pages. No doubt there is some entomologist somewhere who has studied them and could probably tell us a lot more than the average angler knows. I think that this could be of great importance to a considerable number of creative fly tyers. I saw on television once a programme about house flies. A German professor had studied them all his life and still never got round to covering the lot of them and, strangely enough, there are about the same number of different kinds of these too, about 400. I would also think that it is far harder to find out as much about an insect that sometimes exists in its larval stage, often down to 60ft in water, than a land based creature like a house fly.

I used to think that the larva, which is the wormlike creature found usually at the bottom, lashing, as it is most commonly seen, just burrowed into the bottom silt. Since the red ones are generally most conspicuous, I thought that they were all like this, and of course this is not so. They seem to be in a very wide range of colours and sizes from transparent to black, and also from the miniscule to about 2in long, the largest I have seen. I suspect there are probably some even larger. Furthermore, some of the species like the sedge in the larval stage also build themselves little cases to exist in. I found out by observation that they do not always stay in or near the bottom as I have often seen the larvae near the surface, sometimes over deep water but usually at the shallow sides of lakes and ponds. In hot weather conditions they fall prey to surface marauding fish, but remember that the trout is as much a bottom grubber for food as bream is supposed to be, and there is no doubt that most of them are taken at the lower levels.

In the pupa stage they vary in shape so that possibly in every water there are different types to a greater or lesser number as the case may be. I have personally counted, in one evening at Pitsford, at least

The right selection of fly patterns boils down to knowing what is
likely to happen on the water you are fishing.

sixteen different colours and sizes of them at the same time. Allowing
for the fact that this is a reasonably large water, I may have missed more
than a few of the others which were possibly there at the same time. I
have not the knowledge, time nor inclination to study them in great
detail. One has to take a wider view and stick to generalities in that one
basic copy has to cover as wide a range as possible. I rather suspect that
a lot of our imitations do this in fact and it's a damn good job that they
do, because I feel that if the quarry was all that selective, we would have
a much harder job to extract the fish.

This is usually borne out by the fact that many of the traditional flies
that may have been used hundreds of years ago still survive today, and
in their day they would probably catch as many fish as the most recently
invented creations. I write this with tongue in cheek for I believe that
most things in angling are recreated over a period of time and it is
virtually impossible to invent anything new. There is no doubt in my
mind that someone years ago did the same things we are doing today in
one form or another. A few things spring to mind to illustrate this. For
instance, when the sedge pupa begins to be taken, the traditional
Invicta is as good a copy as you will get and the modern version only

scores better in the fact that, in my opinion, it is a much stronger tying of the same thing. Another is the Baby Doll lure which was used as a salmon fly in nearly the same form on the Miranichi river in the States years ago, even describing the wool body that is used today. We all know the follies of tying a fly when new to the game and intending to tie a well known pattern. We then find we do not have the right materials to finish the job correctly and substitute something else. Manage to get a few fish on it and we declare we have invented a new fly and swear by it I intend to take nothing from the many good patterns which have emerged. We should be grateful to their innovators, but to claim one's pattern is new is a very dodgy thing indeed. Years ago, some bright bloke used the same thing and owing to the lack of communication, it never came to light. Not all anglers are very sociable people, and I must confess that there is the odd occasion when I like to do my own thing without interference.

I first started to take an interest in the chironomids which I observed at Eyebrook in the early years, for they were nearly always present in the stomachs of the fish I examined. This soon made me realise their importance as one of the main sources of food in a trout's diet, and also many other fish's as well. I remember that the fish catching qualities of the little Teal and Blacks we used more often than not on the top dropper, started for me one of the most interesting periods of my life. I still haven't finished with them and treat them as the bread and butter of the reservoir trout's menu. In my opinion we haven't come anywhere near to realising their true potential.

It soon became apparent to me that the most obvious (to us) thing about this was the white appendages, the filaments they breathe through. I attempted to copy these by first clipping the wing of a size twelve Teal and Black Short, using this as the pupa, and quite successful it was too. I later tied it with wool in my own crude copies. Another thing that became apparent was the fact that they always seemed to assume a curved shape. This I copied by tying the fly round the bend of the hook and I noticed the underslung head, which I found most difficult to emulate. Nowadays I know how to do it and don't use it. Funnily enough I have turned full circle and gone back to the Spider creations which in a variety of colours have proved far more efficient than all the exact imitations that have evolved since that time.

I went to Blagdon in about 1954 and used my creations to great effect. I saw what the locals there used which, if my memory serves me correctly, was just black silk along the shank with a gold rib rather wide for the size and a tuft of light teal tied back on top of the eye. Mine had a prominent head which I considered at that time to be most important. The one thing I came away with from Blagdon was owing to one chap I spoke to, who showed to me a pale green version which he had found successful during the summer. I came home and started a rethink and tied many more colours and, keeping my eyes open, found out that there were more colours of this type of insect than I had thought possible. As far as we were concerned, they were all classed as gnats. Anything which came and buzzed around your ears was a gnat, a word we don't use much nowadays.

And it was much about this time that a firm called Morrisons put a fly on the market called a Buzzer which was a seal's fur black with a shell back and a white fur head or thorax. This was the first time that I heard the word Buzzer used in conjunction with an imitation of a chironomid. The only other fly I knew was a great big fly used as a chub fly, called a Marlow Buzzer.

I found that my own creations at that time produced a lot of fish from Eyebrook, in the main the black version tending to be the most successful, followed, when the water started to warm up, by the brown job and the green in high summer. The colour popularity varies from water to water and using either the black version or the brown can make a lot of difference in producing fish positively. It does not pay in practice to fish blindly on with one colour if it doesn't produce. You will find that even if many species are on the water, the fish may be interested in just one or two of them.

Things in the chironomid world moved very slowly until the opening of Grafham but since then they have moved rapidly to the present day, and many and wonderful are the creations to represent them. No such bad thing either, but one thing I have found out is that in the struggle to get a more natural presentation, we were going further and further round the bend in more ways than one – reducing the hooking power by blocking the penetration of the point by masking the shank with the dressing. This has turned me back into tying a lot of my flies in a form of low water dressing, allowing a lot of the shank of the hook to remain visible. It doesn't cause any problem whatsoever with their fish attracting abilities. In fact it improves my catch rate considerably, for instead of becoming unstuck after a brief fight, I land every fish that takes hold. I have gradually gone back to tying all my chironomids in Spider form in all the different colours as before. I find tied in this fashion that they are far more versatile because with the addition of more or less hackle they will fish in the attitude I want them to and are far easier to tie. I don't use the curved body for any of the small sizes at all and, what is more, I have found that they produce far more fish this way. I also think that they represent a far wider range of insects in this form for, in the right colours and sizes, they can be taken for the many other things that are taken by trout, including sedges, alders, and other land based insects. Try them, you will not be disappointed I am sure. The last interesting point to do with the bulk of the chironomid family is the fact that their mouth parts are undeveloped and they do not feed in the adult form. This is also true of the much bigger mayfly.

There are of course a lot of other insects which are taken by trout during the course of the fishing season and they all have their time and place. For instance, I know on my local water, Ringstead Grange, that if we get a period of hot weather during the summer, the damosel appears in very large numbers and the large nymphal form of this can take a fair number of fish. The dry fly version of it can be equally successful. Another major food source of lake trout is the freshwater louse which, owing to the great number I find in the stomachs of fish, will be receiving a lot of attention from me in the near future. These can grow quite large, sometimes nearly ½in long and, as far as I know, they do not swim but are usually found around weed beds and crawling along the bottom. With their long legs and antennae, they should provide a challenge for budding fly tyers. I personally think that the introduction of the mayfly into some of our Midland waters would create quite a stir at the end of May and the start of June, not so difficult to do as I found out some years ago from my Irish friends. Even at the moment in the popular angling press there are arguments over the way to do this with one individual saying it's better to catch and transfer the nymph. All I can say is it will take him a long time to catch them as individuals, and by far the better way is to catch the females when they return to the water in a hand net and strip them into water in a container like you strip a trout's eggs and scatter them in the preferred water, because a mayfly can carry about 6,000 eggs. Also if you do the laborious task of transferring the nymph, you cannot be sure it will find the conditions to make a burrow quick enough to get out of harm's way. The Irish too thought about transferring the female full of eggs but decided against this because they thought that owing to predation, they would be taken before the job was done, and furthermore they may have a homing instinct.

The true fact of the Irish experiments was that they reintroduced the mayfly back into a water that had been denuded of them for a few years and after the initial planting of the eggs, they were surprised to find them appearing in quantity the following spring – the biologists had always thought that from the egg to adult stage was a two year cycle. Even they learn more than a little by trial and error. Nature's way of compensation? I think the one lake it should be tried on is Rutland which is on a limestone strata. The little river Guash that ran through the valley had them at one time. The one thing that surprises me a little is the fact that Walker's Mayfly Nymph takes a lot of fish, even in places where there are none present. Still it would be nice to see a hatch of them, like the large Irish lakes I fish.

The olives are insects that feature well in some waters as another source of food and these pretty little creatures, much like a miniature mayfly, occur on quite a few of the waters I fish. The experiences in Ireland taught me how to cope with them a long time ago. They also seem to vary in colour and size considerably. To keep things to basics, I work on the principle that I expect to come across the large variety early on in the season, usually during May if they occur, for over here there are some years when they are very significant by their absence. But if they do appear they can provide exciting sport over a period of a couple of weeks or so. This one is I believe called a lake olive and its size is about half the size of a mayfly and if it does occur, you cannot miss seeing them although the hatch can be very localised. I've seen it on both Pitsford and Grafham, but as I say it does not seem to appear as regularly as it does in the Irish lakes when it always comes on during May.

The smaller varieties, the pond olives, come in a selection of shades in colour from very dark olive, the one in Ireland we call the sooty olive, to a very pale one in high summer, reverting usually back to the dark phase towards the back end. All of them have upright wings and on my local water they have become more prolific in the last two seasons.

My first experience of them was years ago when drifting across Lough Sheelin fishing Black Buzzers and getting quite a few fish. About a half mile downwind I saw great activities of seagulls diving onto the water and great splashing swirls of fish throwing white spray into the air as both birds and fish competed for these large olive flies that were hatching in a very localised area. We pulled our drogue aboard quickly and rowed down to get just upwind of them. I just happened to have a copy in my dry fly box which I immediately put on the top dropper. It was quite large in size, about a ten. I threw it into the activity and instantly had a hard fighting brownie over 3lb. We finished up that afternoon with over seventy fish between us, many of good size, the largest being just over 5lb. Of course we never killed many. I think we took ashore just three. We certainly changed our tactics smartish that day, for once you had drifted through the area two or three times, the action would probably happen about a mile away and we would make a beeline for this, arrive upwind of it and proceed down, getting fish virtually first chuck every time. It certainly got the biggies on the move and a German visitor staying at the Sheelin Shamrock Hotel got one just over 10lb, a beautiful short deep fat fish. If I'd had it I would have had it set up.

It's easy to say you could go through a season and fish with a half dozen patterns and finish up with a lot of fish, which no doubt you could, but when I go on my travels, I carry in excess of 3,000 flies and it's the odd occasion that you need them and if you haven't got them, you wouldn't have half as much fun. I know my boxes of flies have put many fish in the bag which I would not have had without them, especially over the Irish Sea.

The small olive nymph seems to do quite well when the smaller pond olive occurs and, once again, I tie them in different shades. The one simple way of lightening most feather material to a paler colour is to let some of them bleach in a sunny window. If the fish are taking them at the surface, grease up the nymph. Fished in this fashion, they are as effective as a dry fly.

Another insect which occurs periodically is the drone fly which is a creature that looks much like a wasp. When they first appear they frighten most of us, for they will settle on you and are very slow moving. They hatch out of the water and after a time, as happened at both Grafham and Rutland, they are taken by the trout most avidly. It pays to have a reasonably wasp like fly ready in your box when the hatch comes on for when they appear in quantity, the fish will take very little else, and usually the bigger fish come up to take them. They do vary from place to place in colour, some are much darker than others but the artificial I use is an orange to yellow body, ribbed with wide brown bands. It is effective sometimes fished dry, standing up on its hackles. When they appeared on Rutland for the first time, the fish did not like them in this attitude and took them more readily when swamped just under the surface, and this made a lot of difference. I don't think a terrific lot is known about them. That one or two varieties hatch from the larva which is the so-called rat tailed maggot is common knowledge and I have seen them in vast quantities hatching from the sea while cod fishing over the Varne Bank in the middle of the English Channel. They do not sting. They are, however, very spasmodic in appearance and after a good hatch can go years without being seen again.

Appendix

Fly tying instruction has only been given where, in the author's opinion, it is warranted on the grounds of complexity or because the Cove pattern differs from the common commercial patten.

Small Black Spider (2 turn hackle)

Hook: wide gape Partridge; sizes 10, 12 and 14.
Rib: fine silver wire or fuse wire.
Body: black silk or Terylene.
Hackle: black hen (soft) shell; two turns.

The above tying is for normal fishing when used in conjunction with another heavier nymph on as a point fly.

Small Black Spider (3 turn hackle)

Hook: Captain Hamilton Featherweight; sizes 12 and 14.
Rib: as above.
Body: as above.
Hackle: black cock; three turns.

This one is tied to fish high in the water and I generally use it as a top dropper pattern. But if fish are showing regularly and I am having trouble in keeping it close to the surface, I will change to shorter leader 12ft to 14ft, putting two of this type on top and first dropper and using variant number three as point fly.

Small Black Spider (4 turn hackle)

Hook: Captain Hamilton featherweight; sizes 10, 12 and 14.
Rib: as above.
Body: as above.
Thorax: blue underfur of wild rabbit.
Hackle: black cock; four turns.

This one is used as point sometimes greased to keep in surface film to keep the droppers fishing high. It can also with the three or four turns fish as a dry fly. With a little experience you will be able to pick the right combination to suit the water conditions and reaction of fish. The most important thing in all the tyings of the spider is that it is tied reasonably sparse low water fashion, roughly half way to two-thirds along the shank. The fish don't seem to mind a fair bit of metal showing and also three turns of rib visible. This ensures good hooking with the small hooks. Experiment until you find the combinations of hackle and hook weight that suit your own style of fishing.

One further variant that sometimes does well on a very dull day is the Silver Spider tied thus:

Small Silver Spider

Hook: Captain Hamilton featherweight; size 14.
Rib: none.
Body: flat silver.
Hackle: black cock two turns.

For me this is always used as a top dropper pattern.

Small Green and Yellow Spider

This was one of the nymphs that did very well for me in the early days at Eyebrook and has continued to catch fish for me ever since.

Hook: Partridge wide gape; sizes 10, 12 and 14.
Tail: four or five hackle fibres, olive.
Body: rear two thirds pale green silk.
Thorax: yellow silk.
Hackle: small olive.
Rib: silver flat fine tinsel.

VARIANTS

All these patterns are very simple to tie and I usually use the larger sizes in rough water. The best size for general use is size 12.

You will also find that variants of different colours are essential and they vary from water to water. The ones I would suggest in order of my successes are claret, olive, brown and all shades of green. You will probably fill your box with all the different variants and I can assure you they won't be wasted. By far the most important ones are the blacks.

Cove's Pheasant Tail Nymph

Hook: Partridge wide gape down eye; sizes 8 to 12.
Rib: fine copper wire.
Body: ten to twelve fibres (longest you can find), from cock pheasant tail centre.
Thorax: blue underfur of wild rabbit.
Hackle: none.

This pattern is tied well round the bend of the hook. Tying silk any colour tied from eye, right round bend of hook, catch copper wire and pheasant tail fibres pointing towards eye, return silk to three-quarters along shank towards eye, catch pheasant tail fibres, pull straight and take towards eye without twisting them. You should be along the shank in five or six turns. The fibres lie side by side, not on top of one another. Secure with fibres upwards with half a dozen turns of silk. Wind copper wire rib in opposite direction to the fibres, again six turns (the object of the rib is to hold the fibres, not necessarily to be seen), tie in wire and break off wire. Now take a pinch of rabbit underfur and spin on silk, make a small neat round thorax in front of fibres sticking upright. The best way to achieve a good thorax is to wind the fur round on top of itself. When it is to your liking, fetch the upright pheasant tail fibres over the top of thorax at eye of hook, catch with four or five turns of silk, cut off surplus fibres then whip finish. I don't even varnish the tie off. Note, I do not leave a tail, once again this nymph is best tied with a sparse body. Must be tied in all sizes and weights of hooks, and it's probably the most versatile nymph in your box. It's taken thousands of fish in every water.

VARIANTS

In body material only, the different colours in order of importance are green, grey and black. All are tied with dyed swan feather.

Corixa

Hook: Partridge wide gape down eye; sizes 8 to 14.
Rib: silver wire.
Body: white Terylene.

Wing cover: pheasant tail fibres.
Hackle: small brown or white hen.

Take tying silk from eye to hook bend, tie in six to eight pheasant tail fibres with silver wire and Terylene, return silk to eye, make dumpy body with Terylene, tie off then rib with silver wire and break off wire, fetch pheasant tail fibres along back to head, cut off surplus after tying in on top of body, wind three turns small hackle in front, whip finish.

These water boatmen are very versatile bugs to use and although I have personally seen one quite as big as tied on a size 8 hook, I have taken many fish on them and of course there are variants.

VARIANTS

Green Corixa

Hook: Partridge wide gape down eye; sizes 12 and 14.
Rib: silver wire.
Body: white Terylene.
Wing cover: pheasant tail fibres dyed green.
Hackle: green, small.

Silver Corixa

Hook: Partridge wide gape down eye.
Rib: silver wire.
Body: flat silver tinsel.
Wing cover: pheasant tail fibres.
Hackle: small brown hen.

Corixa are mostly fished in sunken ditches, old hedgerows and quiet corners. Also sometimes very productive stalking around the bank fishing very close in.

Sedge Pupa

Of all the sedge pupa patterns I have tried, these two are the most successful:

AMBER SEDGE PUPA

Hook: Partridge wide gape down eye; sizes 10 to 14.
Rib: fine flat gold.
Back: pheasant tail fibres.

Body: amber seal's fur.
Thorax: wild rabbit underfur.

Take tying silk to bend or slightly beyond bend of hook. Tie in pheasant tail fibres and gold rib. Spin on a small pinch of amber seal's fur to just over half way along shank. Fetch gold rib through seal's fur and break off. Bring in fibres and catch in front of seal's fur. Now spin on rabbit fur in front of fibres left sticking upright, making small round head with rabbit fur and bring pheasant tail fibres over the top, once again to eye. Catch in, cut off surplus fibres and whip finish.

This pupa should be left looking reasonably rough with seal's fur poking out at all angles. I am indebted to Peter Grundell of Don's of Edmonton for this pattern.

GREEN SEDGE PUPA

Hook: Partridge wide gape.
Rib: fine gold flat.
Back: pheasant tail fibres.
Body: pale green seal's fur.
Thorax: wild rabbit underfur.

VARIANTS

A wide variety of colours can be tied depending on locality.

Stick Fly

This is the imitation of the larva of the sedge fly which makes itself a case of any available material and crawls about the bottom, dragging its home by its legs and head poking out of the front. I used to think that once in the case, that is where they stayed, laboriously dragging it around. This proves how wrong you can be, because after seeing a most interesting Irish film on sedge larvae, I now know that they are as lively as squirrels, jumping in and out of these cases like things possessed.

Hook: Partridge medium weight nymph hooks; sizes 10 and 12.
Rib: copper wire.
Body: peacock herl, about eight strands tied fairly thick.
Head: cream seal's fur.
Legs: brown hackle.

These cases can vary a lot in colour, depending upon vegetation, sand

and grit available in their environment. It pays to do a bit of observation as to shape, size and colour. Fish will very often take them in mid-water where they can't possibly be naturally. This shows how bright some trout are.

Shrimp

Possibly one of the most available sources of food to most fish in fresh water, and in my view one of the most neglected patterns in modern trout fishing. Nearly all waters contain these and they vary in size, upon my observations from $\frac{1}{4}$-$\frac{7}{8}$in. They seem to vary a lot in colour from dull grey through olive to fawn and, yes, to orange.

Hook: Partridge wide gape; sizes 8 to 12.
Rib: white cotton or silk.
Body: any colour seal's fur within range above.
Back: pale raffine.
Legs: same colour as body, hen hackle.

Wind tying silk to just round bend of hook, tie in first raffine for back, then ribbing, followed by hackle point first. Fetch tying silk back to eye then back again to rear. I do this to ensure strong hold because the raffine can be a little bulky. I then spin on seal's fur to eye, wind the hackle to eye, tie off and cut off surplus, then rib with cotton and cut surplus, moisten raffine and stretch lightly over back and tie off. Cut off surplus raffine. If you've done it right, the raffine forces the hackle downwards to look like the legs and really you don't want too many of them. If you want it to look a little more realistic, tie in a few hackle fibres pointing forwards when you whip finish. Most people I know put a leaded underbody in this pattern. I don't, and especially not in the orange version. Please yourself. I find they hook better without.

Orange Seal's Fur Nymph

This is a creation which sometimes does very well under difficult conditions and for me has attracted better than average size fish.

Hook: Partridge medium weight lure, longshank; sizes 10 and 12.
Rib: flat gold tinsel.
Body: hot orange seal's fur.
Thorax: pheasant tail fibres.

Take silk to bend of hook, tie in ribbing then spin on seal's fur and wind two thirds along shank, then fetch gold rib through this and break off tinsel. Tie in six to eight fibres of pheasant tail on top of shank, spin more hot orange seal's fur in front of this to form thorax, then fetch pheasant tail fibres over the top to eye. Cut off surplus fibres and whip finish. Take out of vice and trim body with sharp pair of scissors to form tapering body

This is sometimes very effective late evening for big rainbows or brownies. Under very good conditions try floating giving an occasional tweak to cause disturbance. Takes can be very violent.

Gold Ribbed Hare's Ear Nymph

Another one that can be very productive under bright conditions, right the way through the season.

Hook: Partridge nymph hooks; sizes 10 and 14.
Body: hare's ear, varying shades.
Rib: fine flat gold.
Hackle: furnace hen.
Tail: a few hackle fibres.

Take silk from eye to bend and tie in tail and ribbing well. Wax silk and spin on hare's ear fibres, taking from tail to eye. Wind rib to eye pulling well in. Break off tinsel and tie in hackle, three turns is plenty. Whip finish.

This nymph can be successful in quite a few sizes on both longshank and normal fly hooks and should be left rough. It can be fished from early season till the end and, according to everything I've ever read, it is supposed to represent the nymph of the pond olive. Whatever it is, it certainly takes more than a few fish and can be used in a variety of ways, even greased up to float in the surface film when sedges are hatching, to right down deep bottom scraping when I rather suspect it is taken as a caddis. I don't worry much what they take it for but when they do they're very confident.

Green Pea Nymph or Farmoor Phantom

Hook: longshank; sizes 10 and 12.
Body: green ostrich herl, centre fluorescent red wool.
Rib: silver wire.

Take tying silk to bend of hook, tie in two or three strands ostrich herl
and ribbing, wind to just short of centre of shank. Now tie in red wool
and wind to make a small ball in centre of hook. Cut off surplus and
wind remaining ostrich herl to eye. Rib and tie off and whip finish.

This pattern was recommended to me by Arthur Smith of Oxford. It
is very useful for rainbows on red hot days.

Pale Green Nymph

This is the nymph that I sometimes use when the caenis is on the water.

Hook: Captain Hamilton medium weight; sizes 12 and 14.
Tail: four or five fibres of olive hackle.
Body: swan wing feather dyed green allowed to bleach in sunny
window to very pale.
Rib: very fine gold wire.

Jersey Herd Nymph

This fly is the very well known creation by Tom Iven which he used
mainly in the larger sizes fished fast as a fry imitation. I find it fishes
better for me on bright early season cold conditions. Crept along dead
slow on or near the bottom it can be very deadly so use it nymph
fashion. And I use a gold tinsel body instead of the copper coloured
milk bottle top that Tom originally used. Tie it small and neat.

Hook: Captain Hamilton medium head; sizes 10 and 12.
Body: flat gold tinsel slightly built up.
Back: eight strand peacock herl.
Hackle: hot orange.

Red Diddy

Hook: Captain Hamilton; size 8
Rib: fine gold wire.
Body: crimson silk.
Tail: part of red rubber band.
Thorax: rabbit fur.

Tie silk to bend, tie in rib wire, prepare rubber band shaved very thin
near the point where it will appear from under the body, dressing later

so that with the natural bend, it is over the top of the hook shank. Take silk back of eye and back to rear again, squashing the rubber band along the shank well down. Now tie in the crimson silk, taking the tying silk back to the eye. Wind the crimson silk back to ⅛in of eye and secure; cut surplus rib and do the same, putting a pinch of rabbit's fur, spin a very small head and tie off. Shave rubber at this point.

Daddy Longlegs

Hook: longshank; size 10. Roundbend; size 10 or 12.
Body: pheasant tail fibres.
Hackle: red cock.
Wing: cree hackle points.

Black Leech

Hook: Captain Hamilton; size 8.
Rib: narrow flat silver.
Body: black wool.
Wing: four hen hackles.
Hackles: black hen.

Take silk to bend and tie in strand of black wool and flat silver ribbing, wind tying silk to within ⅛in of eye, wind black wool and tie off. Cut off surplus, rib in opposite direction to eye, catch and snip off surplus, now pick up the four hen hackles and in sets of two to each side, curving inwards, line them up level and trim off at the quill end and leave them from an inch to an inch and a half long. Tie in over top of body with a dab of varnish at the head to hold the wings securely in place. Best fished very slowly, allowed to get deep, also useful tied in a buff colour.

Dry Grey Buzzer

Hook: Partridge wide gape; sizes 12 and 14.
Body: grey heron herl or dyed swan.
Wing: white hackle points.
Hackle: cock badger, small.

Very useful on a bright day when fish are rising close in and chironomids are on the water. Usually taken with confidence and is used totally as a dry floating on top of the water.

Other fishing books from THE CROWOOD PRESS

Travels with a Two Piece   John Bailey
A collection of writing inspired by the author's journeys along the rivers of England with an ancient two piece fly fishing rod.

River Fishing   Len Head
How to read waters and set about catching the major coarse fishing species.

Boat Fishing   Mike Millman, Richard Stapley and John Holden
A concise but detailed guide to modern boat fishing.

Stillwater Coarse Fishing   Melvyn Russ
A guide to the maze of tackle, baits, tactics and techniques that surround the cream of coarse fishing in Britain.

Beach Fishing   John Holden
A comprehensive insight into the fish, their habitat, long distance casting, tackle, bait and tactics.

In Visible Waters   John Bailey
John Bailey reveals the deep insight that he has gained over nearly thirty years closely observing the lives of the coarse fishing species.

Imitations of the Trout's World   Bob Church and Peter Gathercole
Natural history, physiology, distribution, tackle, tactics and techniques are discussed in this most comprehensive study of the species.

Fly Fishing for Salmon and Sea Trout   Arthur Oglesby
The first recent really comprehensive work to deal almost exclusively with fly fishing techniques.

Tench   Len Head
Natural history, physiology, distribution, tackle, tactics and techniques are discussed in this most comprehensive study of the species.

Pike – The Predator becomes the Prey   John Bailey and Martyn Page
Twenty top pike anglers' experience of all types of waters.

Carp – The Quest for the Queen   John Bailey and Martyn Page
Combined specialist knowledge from twenty-six big fish men.

Long Distance Casting   John Holden
A guide to tackle and techniques of long-range casting in saltwater.

The Beach Fisherman's Tackle Guide   John Holden
Covers rods, reels, accessories, rigs and maintenance.

An Introduction to Reservoir Trout Fishing   Alan Pearson
Covers tackle, casting, flies, bank and boat fishing, and location.

Rods and Rod Building   Len Head
A manual of rod building, giving guidance on design and the selection of rods.

Further information from **The Crowood Press** (0672) 20320